THE LONGEVITY TRAP

The Successful Pre-Retiree's Playbook for Beating Inflation, Making Your Money Last, and Turning Your Extra Decade into the Best Years of Your Life

George McReynolds, CFP®

First Edition

Full title: The Longevity Trap: The Successful Pre-Retiree's Playbook for Beating Inflation, Making Your Money Last, and Turning Your Extra Decade into the Best Years of Your Life

ISBN: 978-1-7372195-6-9

Cover and interior design by: Just Abundance Media LLC

Published by: Just Abundance Media LLC, Telford, PA

Printed in the United States of America

Disclaimer and Disclosure

This book is provided for educational and informational purposes only. It is not intended to provide, and should not be relied upon as, legal, investment, or tax advice. Every individual's financial situation is unique. Before making any decision regarding your pension, insurance, investments, taxes, or estate plan, you should seek the guidance of a qualified professional advisor who is licensed and experienced in those areas. Neither the authors nor the publisher assume responsibility for decisions made without such professional counsel.

Characters and Examples

The examples, case files, and characters in this book are used solely for illustration. Some characters are entirely fictitious. Others are drawn from real-world circumstances but have had names, identifying details, and certain facts changed to protect the privacy of individuals and their families. Any resemblance to actual persons, living or deceased, is purely coincidental.

"I'm getting too old for this."

Sooner or later, we all say it.
The quiet danger of a long life is that your money
will say it first, and run out of road, long before you do.

This book is about making sure it never does.

FOREWORD

I have spent over three decades sitting across the table from people who did everything right.

They saved. They diversified. They listened to every piece of advice the financial industry handed them. And then they retired, relieved, thinking the hard part was over.

It was not over. It was just changing shape.

Years ago, in my own book, The Big Retirement Risk: Running out of Money Before You Run out of Time, I warned readers about the danger that towers over every other one. The true danger is not running out of time. It is running out of money before you run out of time...hence the title of my book. George McReynolds has written the specific playbook for beating it, and he has done something I did not fully appreciate until I read this manuscript. He shows exactly why that risk falls hardest on the very people who did everything else right.

Here is the trap: the more successful you are, the longer you tend to live, and the longer you live, the more time you give five specific dangers room to compound against you. Inflation gets two extra decades to erode a dollar instead of one. A bad sequence of returns in the wrong five years can undo forty years of discipline. Long term care costs do not wait for a convenient moment to show up. Taxes keep compounding right alongside the money. And too often, the spouse who outlives the other is left holding a plan that was never really built for him or her alone. George dismantles each of these five risks, then rebuilds a real answer in their place, a three-bucket income plan that turns a lifetime of saving into an actual paycheck, one that is built to last as long as you do.

I have watched this trap spring shut more times than I can count. A couple retires at sixty-five with a plan that ends at eighty-five, because eighty-five felt safely far away when they built it. Then they turn out to be exactly who they always were, disciplined, well cared for, still playing tennis at seventy-eight, and the plan is suddenly the thing standing between them and the next fifteen years. Nobody plans to be the outlier.

That is the quiet cruelty of longevity. It rewards a well lived life with a longer bill.

I have worked with thousands of financial advisors, and George stands out as one of the best. He built his career defending people, first with his hands as an Army MP, Paramedic and a SWAT officer, then with his mind as a CFP working the full range of the tax and planning world. What you are holding in your hands or on your screen is the same instinct pointed at a new target. He is still defending people. He has just traded a badge for a balance sheet. And he is the rare advisor who understands that the money is only half the job. He writes about it the way clients actually experience it, in stories, not charts, which is exactly why this book will work for the people who need it most.

In the pages of this book, George does something most retirement books never attempt. He asks what all of it was for. In the final third of this book, he turns from money to meaning, from the mechanics of the plan to the purpose behind it, and he draws a distinction every reader should sit with. There is giving with warm hands, while you are alive to see what it does, and there is giving with cold hands, after it is too late to know where the money went and the impact it actually had on the lives and causes you care about.

In the course of my career, I have watched two outcomes, both of which I would consider tragic. The first was someone running out of money years before they ran out of life. And I have watched people who will likely never run out of money, who nonetheless spent their extra decades adrift, having funded a life they never got around to designing. George calls that second failure the trap behind the trap, and he is spot on. A fully funded life that nobody is enjoying, and nobody is giving away while they are alive to enjoy the giving, is still a tragedy. It is just a quieter one.

This book earns the term playbook. It is specific where other books are vague, and it is honest where other books are comforting. If you are an accomplished pre-retiree in your fifties or early sixties, you likely did the saving part right but may be unknowingly planning for the wrong finish line. This is not a book to read once and shelve. It is a book to work through, with your advisor, with your spouse, with an honest accounting of what the years ahead are actually for. The road, as George puts it, is longer than you were told. This book is how you make sure you can afford every mile of it, and then some, with warm hands the whole way.

Erin Botsford

Founder, The Advisor Authority™

Barron's Top 100 Financial Advisor

Author, The Big Retirement Risk: Running out of Money Before You Run out of Time

Advance Praise for

THE LONGEVITY TRAP

"

This book should be required reading for everyone on planet earth. One of our universal challenges is whether our money will outlive us. With gratitude I am living in the extra decade of my life. Living with warm hands instead of cold hands, I have experienced a deeper appreciation of life and humanity. It doesn't get any better than this.

EILEEN CARLIN

Retired Nurse

"

As a single woman with a career in the pharmaceutical industry, one of my goals was to achieve the success necessary to build the wealth to carry me comfortably through retirement. Mr. McReynolds has been my financial advisor for more than 25 years. He reassured me as I transitioned into the uncertainty of retirement nine years ago and has built a solid retirement plan that encompasses the three buckets he outlines in The Longevity Trap: growth, income, and safety. He created a dynamic plan that addresses my wants, needs, and wishes. I have every confidence that with that road map in hand I can keep enjoying the long road ahead. I couldn't have done it without George's guidance.

BONNIE STANKUNAS

Retired Pharmaceutical Regulatory Affairs Director

"

This book is truly a gem. In a light and approachable way, it provides valuable insights into building a durable retirement portfolio and avoiding common pitfalls. But its value extends beyond the technicalities of investment and into the opportunities that abundance can provide, with advice on developing plans to fulfill dreams and a meaningful legacy. This is a must-read for everyone seeking a confident, well-planned retirement.

MICHAEL DEKLEVA

Retired Executive Director, Merck & Co., Inc.

"

This book resonates. I read it cover to cover. It clearly unveils the unavoidable challenges ahead yet includes remedies to best prepare, drawing on your experience alongside two hundred years of financial data. It is slightly daunting, shifting away from the thinking that a more conservative portfolio is the answer nearing and in retirement. The playbook nevertheless shows how to make it less so, and provides a practical approach to prepare in advance for uncontrollable market fluctuations, continue building equity throughout retirement, avoid running out of money, and make the most of a life well planned.

RANDY THEAR

Director, Neuroscience Innovative Medicines Global Regulatory Lead
Teva Pharmaceutical

"

In teaching there is a rule of thumb that students be given the opportunity to learn something three times before they are expected to know or apply it. This Rule of Threes is what George McReynolds has used here. His writing style is conversational and his examples are relatable. There is a lot of food for thought being offered in this book, The Longevity Trap.

JOANNE CLOTHIER

Secondary English Teacher, 1973–2013

"

Another great page turner for all levels of investors. Makes a financially dry subject into an interesting look at YOUR life! See why a 'brilliant' person is not always a good investor. Teaches you to be disciplined in both up and down markets... learn to take advantage of the sales!

JOE KASH

Retired Police Officer | Travel Consultant

"

As usual, George has hit the nail on the head with an eye-opening, factual, tutorial on life itself and the unexpected happenings that come with it. The realization that you may live longer than expected, and outlive your money, is sobering, but George presents it in a way that makes you realize that living longer is a good thing and, with proper guidance, you can be ready for those extra years. Bravo!

CHRISTOPHER CORRADO

Engineer, Inventor, Retired

"

I entered personal finance in 1978 and have counseled many families through every market cycle since. Your book nails the real issue successful pre-retirees face. It shows how the extra decade, or more, as medical science keeps advancing, quietly multiplies inflation, sequence risk, taxes, care costs, and survivor challenges, then gives a practical playbook to turn that longer life into the best years. The income machine framework and stories like Willy and Betty make it actionable. My wife and I are a few years from retirement ourselves with a solid nest egg. This one speaks to us.

DONALD F. MORGAN, AIF®, CPFA®

Lead Planner and Senior Fiduciary Advisor

Independent Wealth Connections Team, Colmina, LLC

"

The Longevity Trap provides a straightforward, yet detailed, strategy for fulfilling a financially and emotionally filling long retirement. George McReynolds succinctly demonstrates the path toward maximizing your retirement nestegg's income potential to confidently allow you to truly enjoy the dollars you worked for all those years.

MARK CACCIATORE

Lieutenant, Philadelphia Police Department, Retired

"

Wow. I am not sure, after reading this book, what hit me more: the goosebumps and the raised hair on my arms when I got to the end and read about warm hands and falling on your back so you can look up, or the fact that my partner of forty-five years could live fifteen years without me.

I wish I had this book twenty years ago. It is written in plain language that is easy to understand and follow. As you turn each page, you want to know more and more.

There is a saying: the Lord writes straight with crooked lines. This book addresses the crooked lines we will assuredly encounter as we live longer and shows how to prepare for them. I did not have this book twenty-five years ago when I was in my mid-forties, but I will make sure my three children and their spouses, who are in their late thirties and early forties, do.

It is entertaining. When was the last time anyone said that about a financial book? It is educational and informative. Well done, easy to read, and it simplifies the complicated.

DAVE BONTEMPO, CPC

The Bontempo Group, Talent Attraction and Retention

"

Contents

INTRODUCTION

The Gift With a Price Tag

Somewhere in your house, there is a retirement book you never finished.

It is not your fault. You bought it with the best of intentions, probably in an airport, probably with a cover photo of a silver-haired couple laughing on a sailboat about something that is apparently hilarious and almost certainly not their tax bracket. You read the first chapter. It told you to save more, spend less, and diversify. You already knew that. So the book migrated to the nightstand, then to the shelf, then to the box in the garage, where it now steadies the short leg of a workbench and is, at long last, doing something useful.

There are, at current count, roughly a gazillion of these books. I have read a genuinely depressing number of them so that you will never have to. Most are written for everyone, which is just a polite way of saying they are written for no one in particular. They ladle out the same reheated statistics, the same lukewarm strategies, the same encouraging pat on the back about opening an account you opened in 1994. They are the oatmeal of the publishing world. Wholesome. Harmless. Immediately forgotten.

This is not that book.

We will not, for one thing, be hauling out the proverbial three-legged stool. You know the one. Social Security, a pension, and your own savings, sketched in every retirement book ever printed as though your future were a piece of patio furniture. I have two small problems with the stool. The first is that you have surely noticed two of its three legs being quietly sawn shorter for years now. The second is simpler. A reader like you did not build what you built by balancing on a stool, and you are certainly not going to fund a thirty-five-year retirement by sitting on one.

I want to make you a promise on this first page. I am not going to bury you in statistics. I will bring you a fact when a fact earns its place, and then I will get out of the way. You did not pick this up to be lectured by a pie chart. You picked it up because some quiet part of you suspects that your situation is not the average situation, and that the average advice therefore does not quite fit. That instinct is correct. Trust it.

Because this book is written for you. Not the statistical blur of you, averaged together with three hundred million other Americans until you come out a sort of neutral beige. The actual you. The one who built something. Who earned well, saved with real discipline, and now stands at the very edge of the thing you spent four decades working toward, holding a large amount of money and a small, nameless unease you cannot quite place.

Allow me to place it for you.

Here is the single sentence this entire book is built around. Read it slowly.

> ***You are going to live far longer than you think, and almost no one, yourself included, has planned for those extra years.***

That is the trap. And it is a strange one, because it is baited with good news.

Here is the good news, delivered once and without a chart. The very things that made you successful, the income, the education, the doctors who actually return your calls, the discipline that had you flossing when you did not feel like it, are quietly buying you extra time. A lot of it. People in your position routinely live ten, twelve, fourteen years longer than the averages that every retirement plan is quietly built on. The finish line you have been running toward for forty years has been moved, in the dark, while you were busy. You trained for a marathon. Somewhere around mile twenty, without a word of warning, they turned it into an ultramarathon.

And nobody planned for those miles.

I see the result of this all the time, and it wears some very familiar faces.

There are Buck and Penny Pincher, who saved like champions their entire lives and now cannot bring themselves to spend a dime of it. They have more than enough. They will tell you, unprompted, exactly how much more than enough. And still they split the early bird entree and drive an extra fifteen minutes for the cheaper gas, not because they must, but because the muscle that saves has grown so strong that the muscle that enjoys has quietly withered. They are not cheap. They are afraid. Nobody told them how long the money had to last, so in their minds it has to last forever, which means it can never be touched.

There is Al Nighter, who cannot fall asleep until the foreign markets open, because if his money is awake, he feels he ought to be too. Every night is an all nighter when your retirement depends on watching a screen at three in the morning.

And there is my personal favorite, a gentleman I will call Mel Thusela, who at sixty-two told me, with total confidence, that he did not need to plan much because the men in his family do not make it much past seventy-five. Mel is now eighty-seven. He is in excellent health, he took up pickleball, and he is, in his own cheerful words, furious about it, because the plan he built for a short retirement is now being asked to fund a long and vigorous one. Mel is the whole book in one man. He is living proof that the pleasant surprise and the financial problem are very often the same event.

Here is what makes the longevity trap genuinely dangerous, and it is the part the oatmeal books miss entirely. A longer life does not simply add good years at the end, like an extra helping of dessert. It stretches every single risk you already carry and hands each one more time to do its work. Inflation gets another two decades to quietly halve your purchasing power, and then start halving it again. Taxes get a longer runway. The cost of care finds its long tail. And a marriage of forty years can become a widowhood of fifteen, with the survivor left holding a tax code and a set of decisions built for two. The extra years do not just need funding. They multiply everything.

If that lands with a small thud in your chest, good. That thud is the most valuable thing you will feel today, because it means you have stopped assuming and started paying attention.

Now let me tell you the part that matters most.

This is the best problem you will ever have.

A long, healthy, well-funded life is the thing human beings have been chasing since we first started keeping track of the years. You are on the verge of getting it. The only thing standing between you and the enjoyment of every mile is a plan built for the actual distance, rather than the one somebody guessed at decades ago. That plan exists. It is not complicated, it is not gloomy, and it does not require you to become someone you are not. It requires you to see the road clearly and then build for its true length.

That is what the rest of this book does. We are going to drive the whole route together, the shadows and the sunrise both. I will show you exactly where the trap is set, why it catches the most successful people hardest, and precisely how to step around it. There will be strategy. There will be specifics. There will, I am afraid, be the occasional bad joke, because we are going to be together for a while and I refuse to hand you a solemn book about the best years of your life.

So here is the only thing I will ask of you. Do not read this one the way you read the last one, the one propping up the workbench. Read it as though it is about you, because it is.

The road is longer than you were told.

Let us go and enjoy every mile of it.

CHAPTER ONE

You Will Live Longer Than You Think

Keith Richards looks like he went to high school with Methuselah.[1] Legend has it a doctor once told him he wouldn't live to see thirty. That doctor has been dead for decades. Keith has not.

[1] Methuselah, grandson of Adam and grandfather of Noah in the Book of Genesis, lived to 969 years of age. Still the record.

Keith is an outlier, obviously. Nobody builds a retirement plan around a man who has spent sixty years defying medicine, gravity, and common sense. But before you file him away as a novelty act, let me guess the number that lives in the back of your mind.

If I stopped you in a parking lot and asked how long you expect to live, you would probably land somewhere in the high seventies. Seventy-eight, give or take...

Here is the problem. For you, that number is not just a little off. It is off by a decade or more, and it is off in the one direction that quietly wrecks a retirement plan. It is too low.

Let me show you why, and let me do it without a single pie chart.

The Number You Are Using Is the Wrong Number

That famous seventy-eight is life expectancy at birth. It is the average lifespan of a baby born this year, and it is dragged downward by every misfortune that can strike a human being between the delivery room and their sixty fifth birthday. It carries the full weight of every tragedy that never touched you. By the simple act of reaching the age you are now, you have already walked past most of the hazards that pull that average down.

So the average at birth is the wrong tool for your job. The number that matters to you is not how long a newborn lives. It is how long someone who has already made it to sixty-five lives. And that number is much larger.

The Social Security Administration, which has a powerful financial motive to count carefully, puts it plainly. A man who reaches sixty-five today can expect to live, on average, to about eighty-four. A woman to about eighty-seven. And those are only the averages. Roughly one in three of today's sixty-five-year-olds will see ninety. About one in seven will see ninety-five.

Now sit with what an average actually contains. That eighty-four for men is the midpoint of everyone who turns sixty-five: the marathoners and the chain smokers, the affluent and the desperately poor, the diligent and the reckless, all thrown into one blender and pureed into a single tidy figure. Half of that group does better than the average. The interesting question, the one that decides how much runway your money needs, is which half you are in.

I suspect you already know the answer. Let me give you the evidence.

I once sat across from a very smart man I will call Norm, which suited him, because Norm had planned his entire retirement around the norm. He had a spreadsheet, and the spreadsheet stopped at eighty. That is the number, he told me, tapping the screen. That is when the average guy checks out. Now, Norm was a nonsmoking, tennis playing, statin taking corporate vice president with two living parents in their nineties. Norm was, in every measurable way, the opposite of average. But he had built his future on the average anyway, because it was the number everyone knew, and there is a strange comfort in planning for the middle even when you have spent your entire life nowhere near it.

It Is Not Only the Money, Though the Money Helps

In 2016, a team led by the Stanford economist Raj Chetty did something no one had managed before. They linked more than a billion tax records to mortality records and mapped, with real precision, how long Americans live at every rung of the income ladder. The study ran in the Journal of the American Medical Association, and its central finding is worth reading twice.

The wealthiest American men outlived the poorest by nearly fifteen years. For women, about ten. A full decade of life, and then some, separating the top from the bottom. That is not a rounding error or a lifestyle footnote. That is the difference between a full second act and no act at all. And it tracked income the whole way up the ladder, not just at the extremes. More income, more years, step after step after step.

If the story ended there, you could tell yourself it is simply about access: better food, better doctors, better neighborhoods. Those things are real and they matter. But the deeper and stranger truth is that money is not the whole of it, and we have known as much for half a century, thanks to a study of people who all had jobs, all had healthcare, and not one of whom was poor.

Beginning in the late 1960s, the British epidemiologist Sir Michael Marmot studied thousands of British civil servants in a body of work now known as the Whitehall studies. These were not slum dwellers. They were office workers in secure government jobs, everyone from the top permanent secretaries down to the messengers and filing clerks. Every one of them could see a doctor. And yet Marmot found a brutally consistent pattern. At every step down the office hierarchy, mortality rose. The messengers died sooner than the clerks. The clerks died sooner than the administrators. The administrators died sooner than the men at the top. It was not a cliff between rich and poor. It was a smooth staircase, and every stair down cost you.

Marmot called it ***the status syndrome***, and its lesson is subtle and profound. It was not only what these people could buy. It was where they stood. How much control they had over their own days. How much autonomy and respect the work afforded them. The person who commands their own calendar tends to outlive the person who answers someone else's bell, even when both carry the same insurance card in their wallet.

You did not merely earn well. You built things, ran things, decided things. You spent a career at or near the top of your own staircase. By Marmot's math, that has been quietly adding years to your life the entire time.

More Years, and Better Ones

Here is where most people brace for the catch. Fine, they think, the successful live longer, but surely those bonus years are the bad ones, spent parked in a recliner with a blanket over the knees. It is a reasonable fear. It is also, mercifully, wrong.

Researchers at University College London followed thousands of older adults on both sides of the Atlantic and measured not just how long people lived, but how long they lived free of disability. The good years. The ones you can actually use. Reporting in 2020, they found that the wealthiest people in their study enjoyed roughly eight to nine more disability free years than the poorest. Not eight or nine more years of decline. Eight or nine more years of the good stuff, of travel and grandchildren and stubbornly winning at pickleball.

This is the distinction that separates the amateurs from the experts in this field, so let me make it clean. *Lifespan is how long you live. Healthspan is how long you live well.* The advantages you have accumulated do not just stretch your lifespan. They stretch your healthspan, and they stretch it further. The extra decade the trap hands you is not a decade of waiting rooms. For someone in your position, it is very likely a decade of Tuesdays worth getting out of bed for. Which is wonderful news, and, as we are about to see, a considerably larger financial problem than a decade of decline would ever have been.

The Odds Get Stranger the Longer You Play

Two more facts, because they bend the math in ways people almost never plan for.

The first is survivorship, and it is delightfully counterintuitive. The longer you live, the longer you are expected to keep living. Your life expectancy is not a fixed appointment on a calendar. It runs away from you as you chase it. A sixty-five-year-old man is aiming at eighty-four. But that same man, once he actually reaches eighty-five, is now expected to see ninety-two. He did not cheat anything. He simply proved, by surviving, that he belongs to the hardier half, and the table adjusts to reflect it. Every birthday you celebrate is also the table quietly revising its guess upward.

The second fact is about couples, and it is the one that quietly undoes more plans than any other. If you are married, you are not planning one lifespan. You are planning the longer of two. And the longer of two runs much further than either alone. For a healthy couple at sixty-five, the odds that at least one of you reaches ninety are better than a coin flip. Plans built around a single life expectancy routinely leave the surviving spouse, most often the wife, funding five, ten, even fifteen years the plan never imagined. We will give that survivor an entire chapter later on. For now, simply notice this: your planning horizon is not your lifespan. It is the last candle on the last cake in your household, and it burns a long time.

Which brings me back to Mel Thusela, whom you met a few pages ago. Mel is the man who assured me at sixty-two that he did not need much of a plan, because the men in his family do not make it much past seventy-five. Mel is eighty-seven now, healthy as a horse, and, in his own words, furious about it. Mel is not a freak of nature. Mel is the rule wearing a party hat. He is exactly what happens when a person who was always going to live a long time plans as though he would not.

This Is *Your* Story

Here is the part I need you to feel, not just read.

Everything in this chapter, the fifteen-year gap, the staircase, the eight extra good years, the coin flip that keeps landing on ninety, is usually served up as a story about other people. A demographic. A cohort. A trend affecting some faceless population of the fortunate.

It is not. It is your story. You are the higher income, higher status, well doctored, disciplined individual these studies keep describing. When the data says the successful live far longer than the average, it is not gossiping about strangers. It is reading your chart aloud. The person most likely to be blindsided by a thirty-five-year retirement is precisely the person most certain that longevity is someone else's story.

So stop using the average. The average is for the average, and you have never been that, not once, not on purpose.

What to Do About It

Insight is worthless until it changes a number on a page, so let me give you the number to change.

First, retire the figure in your head. Life expectancy at birth has no business anywhere near your plan. Replace it with a horizon built for who and where you actually are.

Second, if you are married, plan to the second death, not the first. Build the plan around the longer life, not the average of the two.

Third, get an honest, personalized estimate instead of a gut feeling. Two credible and free tools will do it in about ten minutes:

TWO FREE TOOLS — KNOW YOUR TRUE ODDS

Actuaries Longevity Illustrator — Built by the American Academy of Actuaries and the Society of Actuaries. Designed precisely for couples. Shows you the real odds of reaching each age, not just the average. *longevityillustrator.org*

Dr. Thomas Perls' Living to 100 Calculator — Folds in your own health history, family history, and habits for a personalized estimate. *livingto100.com*

Run them both. Write down what they tell you.

Then, for planning purposes, be generous with yourself. For a healthy, affluent person, building a plan that runs to ninety-five is not pessimism. It is arithmetic. For a healthy couple, running it to one hundred is not vanity. It is prudence. If you overshoot and leave a decade of unused runway, the penalty is a larger legacy for the people and the causes you love. If you undershoot, the penalty is running out of money in a care facility at ninety-three. Those two mistakes are not remotely the same size. When you are unsure which way to round, round up.

This one number, the true length of your road, is the master key to everything that follows in this book. Every strategy in the chapters ahead, every decision about income and taxes and risk and risk management, sits downstream of it. Get the length of the road right, and the rest becomes solvable. Get it wrong, and the finest plan in the world is just a very well-organized way to come up short.

You are going to live longer than you think. Probably not Keith Richards long. But long

Now let us go and find out what that long, wonderful life is quietly going to cost, so that we can pay for it on purpose.

CHAPTER TWO

The Trap Springs

So here is where I ruin the good news.

In the last chapter I handed you a gift. You are going to live a long, healthy, surprisingly vigorous life, quite possibly a decade or more past the number you had been quietly carrying around. Wonderful. Congratulations. Frame it, hang it in the hall, admire it on your way out the door.

Now let me tell you what it costs. Because a gift with a price tag is still a gift. It only turns into a problem when nobody bothers to read the tag. Remember Mel Thusela, eighty-seven and furious about it? Mel got the length of his life right entirely by accident. We are going to get yours right on purpose, and getting it right on purpose means we have to talk about the bill.

Most people picture a longer life as a longer dessert. Same lovely meal, just a bigger slice of pie at the end. If only. A longer life does not gently set a few extra pleasant years onto the back of a plan that was otherwise doing fine. It reaches back into every risk you already carry, every single one, and it hands each of them more time to do its work.

And time, where risk is concerned, is never an innocent bystander. Time is a multiplier.

That is the whole trap, right there. Not the length of the life. The length is the blessing, the very thing we spent all of human history trying to get our hands on. The trap is that the same long road that gives you more sunsets also gives every hazard along it more room to run. You did not sign up for more risk. You signed up for more life. The quiet cruelty of the longevity trap is that, on a spreadsheet, those two purchases look like the exact same transaction.

It is always easier to watch a trap spring on somebody else, so I have brought along two somebodies.

Meet Willy B. Rich and Betty Wont

WILLY B. RICH AND BETTY WONT LIVED ON THE SAME STREET. ONLY ONE OF THEM HAD A MAP.

On one side of the street lives Willy B. Rich. Willy retired at sixty-five with a solid portfolio and one mildly unusual habit. He built his plan for the road he was actually on. His advisor sat him down, showed him a file that looked an awful lot like the last chapter, and told him to plan on seeing his mid-nineties. Willy, being nobody's fool, believed the math and built accordingly.

Directly across the street lives Betty Wont. Betty retired the very same year, with the very same portfolio, into the very same market, blessed with the very same good health. There is exactly one difference between Betty and Willy, and it is not money, it is not luck, and it is certainly not discipline. It is a single number. Betty built her plan around the old, cozy figure that everybody knows. The average. Eighty, give or take. She would be fine, she figured. Probably. Probably is a lovely word. As the cornerstone of a thirty-year retirement strategy, though, it sits somewhere between fingers crossed and how hard can it really be.

You can likely guess where this is heading from their names alone. But the fun, and the lesson, is in watching the trap actually spring. So let us run the tape forward, and let us meet its jaws one at a time.

The Five Jaws of the Trap

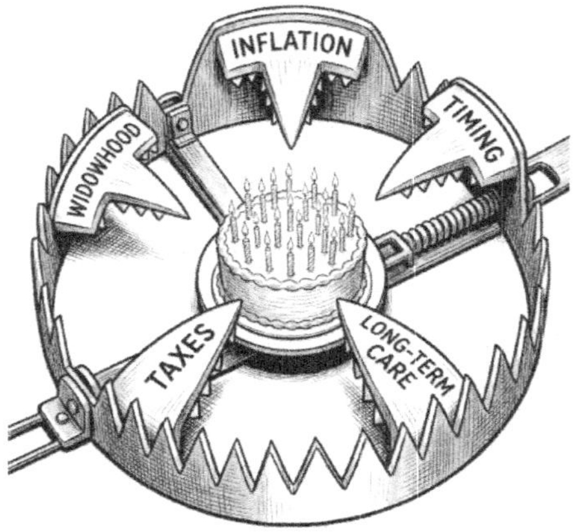

The Longevity Trap has five jaws — and they all bite slowly.

The first jaw is inflation, the silent thief, and the thief does not retire just because you did. Over the long run, prices in this country have climbed by around three percent a year. That sounds almost polite. But at three percent, prices double in roughly twenty-four years. Read that again with your own retirement in mind. Somewhere in their late eighties, both Willy and Betty are standing in a grocery store where nearly everything costs about twice what it did the day they retired. Willy shrugs, because his income was built to climb right alongside prices. Betty's income was flat: perfectly comfortable in her sixties and quietly cut in half by her eighties. Put a number on it. The eighty thousand dollars a year that felt downright generous the day Betty retired needs to be something closer to a hundred and sixty thousand to buy the very same life two dozen years later. Betty planned for the eighty. The other eighty never got an invitation. Same thief. Two very different burglaries.

The second jaw is timing, and it is the sneakiest of the bunch. Early in their seventies, the market throws one of its regularly scheduled tantrums. Willy, who kept a couple of years of spending tucked safely in reserve, simply sips from the reserve and lets his investments recover in peace. Betty, who did not, is forced to sell into the teeth of the decline just to pay her bills, turning a temporary paper dip into a permanent hole in the hull. Professionals have a tidy name for this, *sequence of returns risk*, but you can call it what it plainly is: getting hit at the worst possible moment and then having thirty more years to feel it. A wound in year six of a long retirement has an awfully long time to fester.

The third jaw waits patiently for the late innings.

According to the U.S. Department of Health and Human Services, a person turning sixty-five today runs nearly a seventy percent chance of needing some form of long-term care before the end.

That is not a fringe risk lurking in the fine print. It is a coin flip with the coin weighted against you. In their late eighties, one of our two neighbors needs exactly that sort of care, and it arrives wearing a price tag that runs well into six figures a year. Willy had a line in his plan for precisely this moment. Betty's plan had a blank space where that line should have been, and a blank space has never once paid a care bill.

The fourth jaw is the one almost nobody sees coming, because it is cleverly disguised as good news. Willy and Betty both spent decades faithfully stuffing money into tax deferred accounts, and those accounts kept right on growing, untaxed, deep into their eighties. Here is the catch. The IRS has been a silent partner in those accounts the entire time, and silent partners eventually want a word. The required withdrawals climb as the balance climbs, and the longer you live, the more years there are for that tax bill to swell. Willy began quietly defusing his early, a little at a time. Betty left hers to grow undisturbed, right up until the year those forced withdrawals shoved her into a tax bracket she had not laid eyes on since she was working full time.

The fifth jaw is the quietest, and the hardest. A long life very often means a long widowhood. When one spouse passes, the survivor keeps very nearly all of the household expenses but loses one of the two Social Security checks, often sees a pension reduced or ended, and is shifted out of the roomy married tax brackets and into the cramped single ones, frequently all in the same terrible year. A plan built for two that never once planned for one leaves the survivor to shoulder that shift alone, sometimes for ten or fifteen years. We will hand this jaw an entire chapter of its own later, because it has earned one. For now, simply notice that of all five, it bites the longest.

Same Street, Different Ending

Now step back and look at Willy and Betty from across the street. Same house. Same nest egg. Same market, same health, the same everything a spreadsheet is capable of measuring. One of them glides comfortably into his nineties with money to spare and a legacy to leave behind. The other runs short in her late eighties, anxious and rationing, in the very middle of what was supposed to be a victory lap.

The difference was not returns. It was not luck. It was not even discipline, and heaven knows Betty had discipline to burn. The only difference between these two neighbors was the length of the road each of them planned for. Willy, true to his name, will be rich. Betty, true to hers, wont.

That is the multiplication I keep harping on. Addition, you could have survived. If a longer life simply added risks to your plate one at a time, you could clear them one at a time. But that is not what a longer life does. It takes every risk you already carry and multiplies it by time. And compounding, that same gorgeous force that built your wealth in the first place, works every bit as hard in reverse. It has no opinion about which direction you point it. It cares about one thing only, which is how many years you feed it.

Here is the part that ought to keep you honest. Willy was not smarter than Betty. He was not luckier, and on his worst day he was not one bit more disciplined. He simply refused to plan for a shorter life than the one he was actually going to live. That is the whole trick, start to finish. The longevity trap is almost never sprung by a bad investment or a bad market. It is sprung by thoroughly good people planning, carefully and confidently, for the wrong finish line.

The Good News Hiding in the Bad

So let me say the thing this whole chapter exists to say, and let me say it plainly.

Living longer is not the reward at the end of the plan. It is the stress test the plan was never designed to pass.

Here is why that sentence should leave you hopeful instead of queasy. A stress test is not a verdict. It is a diagnosis. And notice that the entire gap between Willy and Betty came down to one thing: one of them found out about the test with enough time left to study for it. You are, at this very moment, finding out in time.

The rest of this book is the study guide. We are going to take these five jaws apart one by one, inflation, timing, health, taxes, and that long-widowhood, and we are going to build a plan that meets each of them on purpose, with room to spare. The trap only ever springs on the people who never knew it was there. You know it is there now. That single fact changes everything that follows.

You already suspected you were going to live a long time. Now you know what that long life is quietly going to charge you for the privilege.

So let us go and make certain you can afford every wonderful minute of it.

CHAPTER THREE

The Silent Thief Gets Twenty More Years

Why Stock Ownership Is Not the Risk. It Is the Remedy.

In the last chapter, we watched five jaws close on the people who planned for the wrong finish line. This chapter belongs to the first of them, and it is the quietest of the lot. There is an old line from the movies, the weary cop who mutters that he is getting too old for this. Something very like it runs underneath every long retirement, and there are five forces that make yours different from the average person's: timing, healthcare, inflation, taxes, and the survivor left behind to face them alone. Inflation is the one we take apart here, because it is the silent thief, and it is the one almost everyone answers exactly backward. Underneath it sits a question that quietly haunts nearly every person staring down a long retirement, whether they say it aloud or not: how do I make sure I do not outlive my money? It is a reasonable fear. It is also, more often than not, being answered incorrectly.

Most people approaching retirement have spent decades being told to play it safe. They have watched the markets gyrate. They remember the dot-com collapse. They remember 2008. They watched their 401(k) statements with dread, and they quietly resolved that someday, when they finally got to retirement, they would move their money somewhere safe. Somewhere stable. Somewhere out of harm's way.

And that instinct is understandable. It is also, when executed without nuance, one of the most financially dangerous decisions a retiree can make.

Because here is what most people have not been told with sufficient clarity: the enemy of retirement is not stock market volatility. The enemy of retirement is inflation. And the primary weapon we have had for over two centuries against the slow, quiet destruction of purchasing power is equity ownership, stocks.

I want to tell you how I came to write this chapter with particular conviction.

In August of 2024, I attended the LPL Focus conference in San Diego, the annual gathering of some of the most accomplished independent financial advisors in the country. Among the featured speakers was Dr. Jeremy Siegel, the Russell E. Palmer Professor of Finance at the Wharton School of the University of Pennsylvania and the author of *Stocks for the Long Run,* the book that has done more to shape serious thinking about equities and long-run investing than perhaps any other work in the modern era.

I had read the book. I had studied the data. But hearing Siegel speak in person, and having the opportunity to engage with him directly, was a different experience entirely. What struck me most was not the elegance of his argument, though it is elegant. It was his certainty. Not the performative confidence of a man selling something, but the settled, un-defensive certainty of a scholar who has spent decades examining the same evidence from every conceivable angle and arrived at the same conclusion every single time: stocks are not merely a good investment. They are the remedy. The remedy for inflation. The remedy for the slow erosion of purchasing power. The remedy for the very problem that keeps retirees awake at three in the morning.

He presented an updated version of his famous 200-year chart, more current than any edition of the published book, showing the cumulative real returns of stocks, bonds, Treasury bills, gold, and cash stretching from 1802 through 2024. The divergence of those lines over two-plus centuries is so dramatic that the chart almost defies belief on first viewing. Stocks, compounding at roughly 6.7 percent per year after inflation, have produced wealth that dwarfs every other asset class by an order of magnitude. And seeing that chart updated through the end of 2024, after the pandemic, after the worst inflation spike in forty years, after the most aggressive Federal Reserve rate-hiking cycle in a generation, after all of it, the equity line simply continued its long climb, right where two centuries of evidence would have predicted it to be.

That updated chart, and the conversation surrounding it, is the foundation of everything in this chapter. It draws on Siegel's published work spanning three decades and six editions of his landmark book. But it also draws on what I heard and discussed firsthand in San Diego, the living, current version of the argument, from the man who has devoted his career to making it.

We want you to understand this case at a deep level. Not so that you will abandon all caution, but so that you will stop confusing the appearance of safety with actual safety. Bond certificates look safe. Bank CDs feel safe. But feeling safe and being safe, in the context of a 20- or 30-year retirement, are two very different things.

THE INFLATION PROBLEM NO ONE TALKS ABOUT LOUDLY ENOUGH

Let us start with a number. Not a prediction, not a model, a historical fact. Over the long sweep of American economic history, inflation has averaged roughly 3 percent per year. That sounds modest. In any given year, it barely registers. Three percent is what most people round off to zero in their mental calculations.

It is not zero. Over time, it is a wrecking ball.

At 3 percent annual inflation, the purchasing power of a dollar is cut roughly in half in 24 years. A retiree who leaves work at 62, or considerably earlier, and reaches 86, a perfectly plausible outcome given modern medicine and longevity trends, will find that the same $100 they spent in their first year of retirement now requires nearly $200 to purchase the same basket of goods. Their Social Security check will have grown somewhat, but probably not enough. Their pension, if they have one, may be fixed entirely. And their portfolio, if it was invested "safely" in bonds and CDs and money market funds, will have been quietly, relentlessly eroded.

This is what we call the stealth threat. It does not arrive in a dramatic market crash. It does not show up in a single devastating statement. It shows up slowly, over years, in the accumulation of small frustrations: the grocery bill that crept up, the insurance premium that keeps rising, the home repair that costs more than you expected, the Medicare premium that takes a bigger bite than it used to. And one day, a retiree who did everything they thought was right finds themselves stretching their money in ways they never anticipated.

> ***"Inflation is the one risk that bonds leave you exposed to. And it is the one risk that almost always shows up in a 20- or 30-year retirement."***

Dr. Siegel has written extensively on this point, and the data he has compiled going back to 1802 makes the argument with the kind of authority that history alone can provide. The real return on long-term government bonds, adjusted for inflation, has averaged around 3.6 percent per year. Treasury bills have averaged approximately 2.5 percent. Gold, so often held up as the great inflation hedge, has returned just 0.6 percent per year in real terms over that same period. And the dollar itself? The purchasing power of the U.S. dollar has declined at an average rate of 1.4 percent per year going all the way back to 1802.

Meanwhile, the real return on stocks, equity ownership in American businesses, has averaged between 6.6 and 7 percent per year over that same 200-plus-year period. That is not a prediction. That is not a model. That is a data set that has survived the Civil War, two World Wars, the Great Depression, the stagflation of the 1970s, the dot-com bust, the financial crisis of 2008, and a global pandemic.

6.7 percent real. Year after year. Decade after decade. Century after century.

6.7%	*Average annual real return on U.S. stocks since 1802, through every war, crisis, and recession the nation has faced. (Siegel, Stocks for the Long Run, 6th Ed.)*

Compare that to the alternatives. At 2.5 percent real from Treasury bills, your purchasing power doubles roughly every 28 years. At 3.6 percent real from long-term bonds, it doubles in about 20 years. At 6.7 percent real from stocks, purchasing power doubles approximately every 11 years. For a retiree facing a 25-year retirement, that difference is not academic. It is the difference between a comfortable late life and a frightening one.

THE TWO CENTURIES OF EVIDENCE

One of the most powerful contributions of Siegel's work is its refusal to cherry-pick time periods. It is easy for an advocate of any investment class to find a favorable 10- or 15-year window that proves a point. What is far harder, and far more meaningful, is a data set that spans more than 200 years, encompasses every imaginable economic environment, and still tells a consistent story.

That is what Siegel provides. And the story it tells about stocks is remarkably stable.

The Three Eras of Stock Market Returns

Siegel divides American financial history into three broad periods, and the consistency across them is striking:

Era	Period	Real Annual Return
Early America	1802 to 1870	6.7%
Industrial Expansion	1871 to 1925	6.6%
Modern Era	1926 to 2021	7.1%
Full Period	1802 to 2021	6.9%

Think about what is embedded in those numbers. The period from 1802 to 1870 includes the War of 1812, the Panic of 1837, the Civil War, and multiple regional financial crises. The period from 1871 to 1925 includes the Panic of 1873, the Panic of 1893, the Panic of 1907, and the worst pandemic in modern history, the 1918 Spanish flu, which killed between 50 and 100 million people worldwide. The period from 1926 to 2021 includes the Great Depression, World War II, the Korean War, the Vietnam War, the stagflation of the 1970s, Black Monday in 1987, the S&L crisis, the dot-com collapse, the worst financial crisis since the Depression, and a global pandemic that shut down the global economy for months.

And through all of it, the long-run real return on stocks stayed within a remarkably narrow band: 6.6 to 7.1 percent per year.

Dr. Siegel himself, when interviewed for the sixth edition of his book, put it simply: "I updated the data to June of this year and it's 6.7% real, exactly the same as 30 years ago, despite the financial crisis, COVID, and so forth. It's remarkably durable."

Remarkably durable. That is perhaps the most important phrase in this entire discussion. Not "occasionally good." Not "superior in some decades." Remarkably durable. Across wars, panics, pandemics, technological revolutions, and political upheavals that would have seemed unimaginable to any investor living through them.

What the Competition Looks Like Over Time

To understand why the stock return story is so compelling, it helps to compare it concretely against the alternatives that retirees typically gravitate toward:

Asset Class	Real Annual Return (1802-2021)	Purchasing Power Doubles In
U.S. Stocks (equities)	6.9%	~10.5 years
Long-Term Gov't Bonds	3.6%	~20 years
U.S. Treasury Bills	2.5%	~29 years
Gold	0.6%	~117 years
U.S. Dollar (cash)	-1.4%	Never, declines

That last row deserves its own moment of silence. Cash, the thing people move into when they want to be "safe", has lost purchasing power at a rate of 1.4 percent per year on average across American history. A retiree who keeps a significant portion of their assets in cash or near-cash equivalents is not playing it safe. They are accepting a slow, certain loss as their defense against a possible temporary one.

Siegel's conclusion on this point is almost jarring when you first encounter it: when long-term purchasing power is considered, stocks are actually safer than bank deposits. Not safer in the sense that they do not fluctuate, they clearly do. Safer in the sense that they are far more likely to preserve and grow the real purchasing power of your money over the horizon that actually matters in retirement planning.

WHY STOCKS WIN AGAINST INFLATION: THE MECHANISM

Understanding what the data says is one thing. Understanding why it says it is another, and the why matters enormously, because the why is what turns grudging compliance into genuine conviction. And conviction is what keeps you in your seat when the headlines are screaming at you to run.

Stocks are not just pieces of paper that go up and down on a screen. A share of stock is a fractional ownership interest in a living, breathing, adapting enterprise. It represents a claim on real assets, factories, patents, land, equipment, software, brands, customer relationships, intellectual property. And crucially, it represents a claim on the earnings those real assets generate.

When inflation rises, prices rise. The grocery store charges more for the food it sells. The pharmaceutical company charges more for the drugs it manufactures. The technology company raises subscription prices. The energy company earns more for each barrel of oil it produces. And those higher prices flow through to higher revenues, and over time, to higher earnings, and therefore to higher stock prices and higher dividends.

This is the fundamental mechanism that makes equities an inflation hedge in a way that bonds simply cannot be. A bond is a fixed contractual promise: you lend money, you receive interest at a fixed rate, and you get your principal back at maturity. That interest payment does not increase when inflation rises. That principal does not grow when the economy expands. The bond is a snapshot of the purchasing power of the moment it was issued, frozen in time, slowly being eroded by the rising price level around it.

"A bond is a frozen promise. A stock is a living claim on the future. Only one of them can keep pace with inflation."

Stocks, by contrast, are a dynamic claim on the future earnings of businesses that will adapt to, and often profit from, inflationary environments. When a well-run company faces rising input costs, it raises its prices. When wages rise throughout the economy, a dominant business raises its prices too, and often comes out ahead because its pricing power exceeds its cost increases. The great businesses of the world, the ones that are diversified across an index fund or a thoughtfully managed portfolio, do not sit passively while inflation erodes their margins. They fight back. And over time, they win.

This does not mean stocks are immune to inflation in the short run. They are not. In fact, unexpected spikes in inflation can roil equity markets significantly in the short term, because higher inflation often leads to higher interest rates, which compress the valuations investors are willing to pay for future earnings. The 1970s are the canonical example: stocks struggled mightily during the period of peak inflation, producing negative real returns for much of the decade.

But here is the key word: short run. Over 10, 15, 20, 25, and 30-year periods, the periods that actually matter for retirement planning, stocks have consistently, reliably, and by a wide margin outpaced inflation. The short-term volatility that frightens investors is, from a long-run perspective, simply the noise that surrounds a very powerful signal.

The Danger of Confusing Volatility with Risk

This is one of the most important distinctions in all of personal finance, and it is one that the financial media has almost completely failed to communicate clearly. Volatility and risk are not the same thing. They feel the same, but they are fundamentally different concepts.

Volatility is the fluctuation in the price of an asset over time. Risk, in the context of retirement planning, is the probability of permanent impairment of your purchasing power, the probability that your money will not do what you need it to do over your lifetime.

A stock portfolio is highly volatile. Its value will go up and down, sometimes dramatically, from quarter to quarter and year to year. This volatility is uncomfortable. It is psychologically difficult. It tests conviction. But for an investor with a long enough time horizon and a well-diversified portfolio, this volatility is not risk in the meaningful sense. It is the price of admission to the higher long-run returns of stocks.

A CD or a government bond is not volatile in the traditional sense. Its price does not swing. Its stated return is predictable. But for a retiree who needs their money to last 25 or 30 years, a portfolio that is heavily weighted toward fixed instruments is profoundly risky, it just happens to be risky in a way that is quiet, gradual, and therefore emotionally tolerable. We are much better at tolerating slow death than fast pain, even when the slow death is more certain.

Siegel puts it this way: stocks have returned an average of roughly 6.5 to 7 percent per year after inflation over the last 200 years. Over any 20- to 30-year holding period in that data set, stocks have virtually never failed to beat bonds and cash. The short-run volatility, which is what investors fear and what drives them to seek the apparent safety of bonds, essentially disappears when viewed over the long run. The risk of holding stocks too long, in other words, is far smaller than the risk of not holding them long enough.

WHAT BONDS CAN AND CANNOT DO

We want to be careful here, because this chapter is not an argument that retirees should have no bonds, no fixed income, no stable assets in their portfolio. That would be reckless and wrong. The argument is more precise: bonds serve specific and valuable purposes in a portfolio, but hedging against inflation over a long retirement is not one of them. And far too many retirement portfolios have been structured as if it is.

Here is what bonds are genuinely good for:

- Providing stability and ballast during equity market downturns, so you do not have to sell stocks at depressed prices to fund near-term living expenses.
- Generating income in the form of interest payments that can supplement other income sources.
- Reducing overall portfolio volatility so that investors can stay the course emotionally during turbulent markets.
- Serving as a liability-matching tool when you have known, fixed expenses at known future dates.

These are real benefits. They matter. A portfolio with no bonds or fixed income at all is difficult for most retirees to hold through a major market downturn, and the investor who panics and sells at the bottom does far worse than the investor who held an 80/20 or 70/30 portfolio and stayed put.

But here is what bonds cannot do, and this is where Siegel's analysis is at its most piercing: bonds cannot preserve your purchasing power against inflation. They are, in fact, uniquely vulnerable to it.

When inflation rises, interest rates tend to rise as well, because lenders demand compensation for the erosion of the purchasing power of the dollars they will receive back at maturity. When interest rates rise, the price of existing bonds falls, sometimes dramatically. A long-duration bond portfolio can lose 15 to 30 percent of its value during a significant interest rate cycle, which is the kind of loss that would cause significant alarm if it happened in a stock portfolio but somehow gets classified differently when it happens in the bond portfolio.

The 2022 bond market gave American investors a visceral taste of this reality. In a year when many equity investors expected bonds to provide shelter from a volatile stock market, the Bloomberg U.S. Aggregate Bond Index, the most widely tracked bond benchmark in the country, fell approximately 13 percent. Combined with the equity decline that year, many supposedly "conservative" balanced portfolios posted their worst performance in decades. The very thing investors held bonds to hedge against, large portfolio drawdowns, materialized anyway, because the driving force was inflation and rising rates, which hit bonds just as hard as stocks.

As Siegel himself observed in commentary following that period: "There is one sort of risk that a bond cannot deal with, and that is inflation. And that is what has exploded over the last two or three years since the pandemic. Bonds have not become a good hedge, and that is a major reason why bond rates have gone back to the levels we had pre-financial crisis."

~13%

The loss suffered by the Bloomberg U.S. Aggregate Bond Index in 2022, the same year many investors expected bonds to provide safety from inflation-driven market volatility.

THE RETIREMENT EQUITY IMPERATIVE

Let us now bring this directly into your retirement, because the implications are significant and, in my experience, frequently misunderstood, even by professionals who ought to know better.

Here is the planning reality: if you retire at 65 and live to 90, a 25-year retirement, you need your portfolio to survive and grow in real terms for a quarter century. And if you retire earlier, as many public safety professionals do at 50 or 52, and as pharmaceutical and corporate executives often do at 55, that horizon stretches to 35 or even 40 years. The math does not get more forgiving. It gets considerably more demanding. That is not a short investment horizon. That is not an emergency fund. That is an investor with a 25-year time horizon who happens to also be making withdrawals.

The traditional model of retirement portfolio construction said: as you get older, shift more of your portfolio into bonds. There was logic behind this at a time when retirement lasted 10 or 12 years. There is far less logic behind it today, when a healthy 65-year-old couple has a roughly 50 percent chance that at least one partner will reach 90.

What does 25 years of 3 percent inflation do to purchasing power? It reduces it by nearly 50 percent. A retiree who needs $10,000 per month to live comfortably at 65, or at 55, will need roughly $19,000 per month to maintain the same lifestyle at 90, assuming 3 percent average inflation. If their portfolio is heavily allocated to bonds and cash generating a real return of 1 to 2 percent, it will be fighting a losing battle against that inflation tide. If their portfolio holds a meaningful allocation to equities generating 6 to 7 percent real, they have a genuine shot at maintaining and even growing their purchasing power across the full span of retirement.

"The question is not whether you can afford the volatility of stocks. The question is whether you can afford the certainty of inflation without them."

Siegel makes this argument with particular force in *Stocks for the Long Run,* noting that those accumulating savings for retirement should allocate a more significant portion of their portfolio to equities, given their longer investment horizon. This is not a controversial view in academic finance. It is not a fringe position. It is the conclusion that emerges from one of the most comprehensive empirical investigations into asset class returns ever conducted.

The challenge is not intellectual. It is emotional. And it is exacerbated by the way financial news is presented, the way market downturns are covered, and the way the financial services industry has historically packaged and sold "safe" retirement solutions, often prioritizing what feels good over what works.

A Fair Objection About Timing

At this point, a sharp reader raises a fair objection: what about a bad market right at the start? A steep decline in the first years of retirement, when the portfolio is at its largest and the withdrawals are just beginning, can do lasting damage that the very same decline would not do a decade later. This is called sequence of returns risk, and it is entirely real. It is not, however, a reason to abandon equities. It is a reason to hold them inside a structure that never forces you to sell into a falling market. That structure exists, and because it is the whole difference between a plan that survives the fragile years and one that quietly does not, it has earned a chapter of its own. It is the very next one. For now, hold two thoughts together: you need stocks to beat the thief, and the timing of their worst years can be managed rather than feared.

THE PSYCHOLOGICAL BARRIER: WHY SMART PEOPLE FLEE TO SAFETY

"To invest successfully over a lifetime does not require a stratospheric IQ, unusual business insights, or inside information. What's needed is a sound intellectual framework for making decisions and the ability to keep emotions from corroding that framework."

WARREN BUFFETT

It would be dishonest to pretend otherwise, so let me say it plainly, because I watch it happen again and again: the case for owning stocks in retirement is intellectually simple and emotionally brutal.

People who have spent 30 or 40 years accumulating assets have a very different relationship to their portfolio than they did when they were 35 and still earning. When you are earning, a market decline is an opportunity: stock prices are lower and your next paycheck will buy more shares. When you are withdrawing, a market decline feels like a threat to everything you have built. The psychological experience is profoundly different.

Add to this the media environment that surrounds investing. Market declines are front-page news. They are covered with urgency, alarm, and graphic imagery. Market recoveries are reported as a footnote.

The result is that the investing public has an enormously distorted perception of the frequency and permanence of market downturns. They remember the crashes vividly and discount the recoveries.

In behavioral finance, this is called loss aversion, the well-documented human tendency to feel the pain of a loss roughly twice as intensely as the pleasure of an equivalent gain. It is not a character flaw. It is a feature of the human brain that may well have served us well on the savanna but does not serve us well in a long-run investment context.

Daniel Kahneman, the Nobel Prize-winning psychologist and economist, documented this phenomenon extensively. Shlomo Benartzi and Richard Thaler extended this work to show that *the frequency with which investors evaluate their portfolios significantly affects their risk tolerance:* ***investors who check their statements monthly feel the pain of interim volatility far more acutely than those who evaluate annually***, and are far more likely to make decisions driven by that pain rather than by long-run logic.

KEY INSIGHTS: The Psychology of Investment Decisions

Loss Aversion

The pain of a financial loss is felt roughly twice as intensely as the pleasure of an equivalent gain. This is not a character flaw, it is a feature of the human brain. Understanding it is the first step toward overcoming it.

The Savanna Problem

Our instinct to flee from danger served our ancestors well. It does not serve the long-run investor. The brain that kept us alive on the savanna is the same brain that sells equities at the bottom of every market cycle.

How Often You Look Determines How Much You Fear

> *Investors who review their portfolios monthly experience significantly more pain, and make significantly more fear-driven decisions, than those who evaluate annually. The frequency of evaluation is itself a risk management variable.*

This is why a sound plan matters far more than good intentions. Left to our own devices, even the most intelligent and accomplished among us will reliably reach for the choice that is emotionally comfortable and financially inferior. The purpose of a plan is not to override your emotions. It is to build something sturdy enough that your emotions cannot knock it over.

"Your instinct to seek safety is not wrong.

Your definition of safety may be."

THE VALUE OF DIVIDENDS: A FORGOTTEN PILLAR

One of the most underappreciated aspects of the long-run equity return story is the role of dividends. In Siegel's analysis, dividends are not a minor feature of stock ownership. They are, historically, the primary driver of long-term stock market returns.

Consider this: over the long sweep of market history, ***approximately 40 to 50 percent of the total return from stocks has come from dividends and dividend reinvestment, not from price appreciation alone.*** The investor who holds stocks for their dividend stream and reinvests those dividends during periods of market weakness is systematically buying more shares at lower prices, compounding their ownership stake in a way that pure price appreciation does not capture.

For a retiree, dividends serve a second critical function: they provide income without requiring the sale of shares. A portfolio with meaningful dividend income allows a retiree to fund a portion of their living expenses simply by collecting and spending the dividends their holdings generate, leaving the underlying principal intact to continue compounding and growing. This is particularly valuable during periods of market weakness, when selling shares to fund expenses would mean locking in losses.

The *Dow 10 strategy (the Dogs of the Dow)*, holding the 10 highest-yielding stocks in the Dow Jones Industrial Average and rebalancing annually, is one of the dividend-focused approaches Siegel discusses in some detail. While no single strategy is right for every investor or every market environment, the underlying point is powerful: dividend-paying stocks are not just *growth* instruments. They are *income* instruments as well, and the combination of growth potential, dividend income, and the ability to keep pace with inflation makes them uniquely suited to the needs of a long-lived retiree.

International diversification adds another dimension to this story. Siegel's work on global markets demonstrates that the equity premium, the advantage of stocks over bonds and cash, has not been unique to the United States. It has appeared across developed markets around the world, with variations in magnitude but not in direction. A globally diversified equity portfolio captures multiple streams of economic growth, multiple dividend traditions, and multiple currency exposures, reducing the reliance on any single market's performance and smoothing the overall return profile.

ADDRESSING THE OBJECTIONS

When people first hear this evidence, a handful of objections come up almost every single time. Let us meet them head on.

"But what if the market doesn't recover this time?"

This is the question that haunts every investor who has been through a major decline. And it is worth taking seriously. The honest answer is: it is possible that any specific 10-year period will see disappointing equity returns. It is even possible, though historically rare, that a 20-year period will underperform. What is vanishingly unlikely, based on 200-plus years of data, is that a diversified equity portfolio held for 25 to 30 years will fail to significantly outperform bonds and cash in real terms.

The objection, at its core, is a claim that "this time is different", that the conditions that have driven equity outperformance for two centuries have fundamentally changed. That claim is possible. It is *not* historically supported. And it is worth noting that this objection has been raised at every major market peak in modern history, and has been wrong every time.

"I can't psychologically handle seeing my portfolio fall 30 percent."

This is a different kind of objection, and it deserves a different kind of answer. This is not really an objection to the data. It is an acknowledgment of a real human limitation. And it is one of the most important conversations we can have with clients.

The answer is not to abandon equities. The answer is to build a portfolio structure that makes the short-term volatility of the equity portion emotionally survivable. That means ensuring there are sufficient liquid reserves to fund three to four years of living expenses without touching the equity portfolio. It means designing a withdrawal strategy that does not require selling stocks at depressed prices. And it means, sometimes, using specific protective strategies, like the registered index-linked annuities we will explore in their own chapter, to provide a defined downside buffer that makes equity-like exposure more psychologically manageable.

Our goal is not to convince clients to feel something they do not feel. The goal is to build a financial structure that is robust enough to do its job even when, inevitably, the client's emotions are pulling in a different direction.

"My neighbor lost everything in the stock market."

Anecdote is powerful. It is also, in this context, almost always misleading. "Lost everything" in the stock market means one of two things: either the investor sold during a decline and locked in losses that would have recovered, or the investor was not diversified and held concentrated positions in individual stocks that permanently failed. A diversified, low-cost, long-held equity portfolio has never "lost everything" over any meaningful long-term period in American financial history. The stories of catastrophic loss in the stock market are almost invariably stories of concentration, leverage, or panic selling, not stories of patient, diversified, long-run equity ownership.

"Rates are high enough now. Why take the risk?"

This objection has appeared with particular force in 2024 and 2025, as interest rates have moved to levels not seen since before the financial crisis. A 5 percent Treasury bill yield or a 5 percent CD rate sounds very attractive compared to the yields available in 2020 or 2021. And for short-term money, funds that will be needed in one to three years, high-quality, short-duration fixed income is genuinely the right tool.

But for a retiree whose money needs to last 25, 30, or even 40 years, the relevant question is not what return is available today. It is what return will be available over the next 25 years, and more importantly, what real return will be achieved after inflation over that full period. High nominal rates in the current environment largely reflect elevated inflation expectations. Real yields, the return above inflation, remain far below what equities have historically delivered. Locking a 30-year retirement into today's nominal yields without equity exposure is a bet that inflation will be permanently subdued and that equities will disappoint over the long run. That bet has lost, repeatedly and badly, for every investor who has placed it throughout American financial history.

A FRAMEWORK FOR THE EQUITY-COMMITTED RETIREMENT PORTFOLIO

All of this leads naturally to the question of what a well-constructed retirement portfolio actually looks like when we take the inflation evidence seriously. Let us sketch the framework, with the understanding that every client's situation is different and that the principles here must be adapted to individual circumstances, risk tolerance, time horizons, and income needs.

The Core Equity Allocation

For a retiree with a 20-plus-year time horizon, a meaningful equity allocation is not optional, it is a planning necessity. What constitutes "meaningful" will vary by individual. A rule of thumb that has become more defensible in light of modern longevity data is the 100-minus-age allocation (allocate a percentage equal to 100 minus your age to equities). Some planners have revised this to 110 or 120 minus age, reflecting the longer life expectancies of modern retirees.

A 55-year-old retiree from public safety or a pharmaceutical career, with potentially 35 or more years ahead, might reasonably carry 65 to 75 percent in equities. A 65-year-old might carry 50 to 65 percent. A 70-year-old might carry 40 to 55 percent. These are not universal prescriptions, they are starting points for a conversation about what allocation allows a specific client to stay invested through market turbulence while still providing the long-run growth necessary to outpace inflation over a retirement that may last far longer than the average.

Within the equity allocation, diversification across market capitalizations (large, mid, and small), styles (growth and value), geographies (domestic and international), and sectors reduces concentration risk without reducing the long-run return potential that makes equities valuable.

The Liquidity Reserve

The equity allocation is safeguarded, psychologically and practically, by a liquid reserve sufficient to fund two to four years of planned withdrawals without selling equities. This reserve is held in cash equivalents, short-duration bonds, or other highly liquid, low-volatility instruments. It is not expected to generate inflation-beating returns. It is expected to help the retiree stay invested and resist the temptation to sell equities at a loss during market downturns.

The liquidity reserve is replenished periodically from equity gains during periods of market strength, maintaining the structural separation between the short-term spending account and the long-term growth portfolio.

The Income Layer

Between the liquidity reserve and the growth equity portfolio, many retirees benefit from an income layer: dividend-focused equities, real estate investment trusts, or other instruments that generate current income without requiring the sale of shares. This income layer reduces the annual withdrawal burden on the equity portfolio, extends its longevity, and provides a cushion of income that continues even when equity prices decline.

For anyone who finds pure equity exposure emotionally difficult to hold, this is also where structured products like registered index-linked annuities, which earn a full chapter of their own, can play a valuable role. By reducing downside risk while maintaining meaningful upside participation, these products can serve as a bridge between the emotional need for risk reduction and the financial need for growth. They will not deliver the full upside of unconstrained equity ownership. But they can deliver equity-linked growth with a defined floor, which for some investors is the difference between staying invested and fleeing to cash at the worst possible moment.

THE INTEGRATED VIEW: WHAT SIEGEL'S WORK REALLY TELLS US

Jeremy Siegel's *Stocks for the Long Run* is, at its core, an argument for intellectual honesty about investing. It is an argument against the comfortable fiction that safety looks like stability, that bonds are safe because they do not fluctuate, that cash is safe because it does not lose nominal value.

What Siegel shows us, with more historical evidence than perhaps any other single work in personal finance, is that a retirement built to last, the kind that actually preserves your purchasing power over a long retirement, looks very different from what it feels like. It requires the willingness to accept short-term volatility in service of long-run real return. It requires the intellectual discipline to look past the market headlines of any given week or quarter and keep faith with a strategy that has worked, without exception at the multi-decade level, for over two centuries.

My decade as a first responder taught me this about human nature:

Human beings are not built to think in twenty-year time horizons. Our brains are wired to respond to the immediate threat, the loud bang, the market drop, the frightening headline, the neighbor who lost everything.

The job of a good plan is to be the steady counterweight to those instincts, not by dismissing them, but by being robust enough to survive them.

The good news is that the data is extraordinarily encouraging. You do not have to find the right stock. You do not have to time the market. You do not have to make brilliant investment decisions. You have to own a diversified portfolio of equities, maintain appropriate liquidity reserves, manage the emotional temptation to flee during downturns, and give the mathematics of compounding real returns the time it needs to work.

Two hundred years of data says that is enough. Not in every 5-year period. Not in every 10-year period. But over the long run, the actual run of a modern retirement, it has been enough. Consistently. Durably. Without exception.

> ***"The cast stabilizes the broken bone. The body heals it. Patient equity ownership is the cast that holds a retirement together while the long-run math does its work."***

CONCLUSION: THE INFLATION IMPERATIVE IS NOT OPTIONAL

We began this chapter with a question: how do you make sure you don't outlive your money? The answer that emerges from 200-plus years of financial history is not complicated, even if it is emotionally challenging.

You own businesses. You own them broadly, through diversified equity portfolios. You own them patiently, through market cycles that will test your conviction and try your patience. You preserve your short-term liquidity so that you are never forced to sell your long-term investments at the wrong time. And you give the mathematics of real return compounding the time it needs to work in your favor.

Inflation is the enemy. It is slow, it is patient, and it is certain. The only durable, historically validated answer to it is equity ownership. Everything else, the bonds, the CDs, the money market funds, the gold, has a role to play, but none of them can lead your portfolio. None of them can deliver the 6.7 percent annual real return that stocks have delivered, across two centuries and every imaginable adversity, to investors who had the discipline to stay invested.

The question you need to ask is not whether you can handle the volatility of stocks. It is whether you can afford the certainty of inflation without them.

Understanding this, truly understanding it, is some of the most valuable financial thinking you will ever do, because it changes the one decision that every other decision in your retirement quietly depends on.

There is one more piece to this, and it is important enough to stand on its own. Owning enough stocks to outrun the thief only works if a brutal market in the wrong year does not force you to sell them at the bottom. That danger, the risk of terrible timing in the fragile years right around your retirement date, is real, and it is the subject of the very next chapter. Later in the book, once we have named both of these dangers plainly, the slow thief of inflation and the sudden ambush of bad timing, we will look at a modern tool, the registered index-linked annuity, that was built to soften both at once.

Sources and Further Reading

Siegel, Jeremy J. *Stocks for the Long Run*: The Definitive Guide to Financial Market Returns and Long-Term Investment Strategies, Sixth Edition. McGraw-Hill, 2022.

Siegel, Jeremy J. "Why Stocks Will Remain Strong in the Long Run." Knowledge at Wharton, October 2022.

Siegel, Jeremy J., and Richard Thaler. "Anomalies: The Equity Risk Premium." Journal of Economic Perspectives, 1997.

Kahneman, Daniel. Thinking, Fast and Slow. Farrar, Straus and Giroux, 2011.

Benartzi, Shlomo, and Richard Thaler. "Myopic Loss Aversion and the Equity Risk Premium." Quarterly Journal of Economics, 1995.

U.S. Bureau of Labor Statistics. Consumer Price Index Historical Data, 2025.

Bloomberg. U.S. Aggregate Bond Index Annual Returns, 2022.

CHAPTER FOUR

The Ambush

The last chapter was about a thief who works slowly. This one is about an enemy who works all at once.

Inflation is patient. It robs you a few percent a year for thirty years and never once raises its voice. The danger in this chapter is its opposite in every way. It is sudden, it is loud, and it does not need thirty years to do you in. It needs one, if it picks the right one. It lies in wait for a single moment, the most vulnerable moment of your entire financial life, and it strikes there. I call it the ambush.

And here is what makes the ambush so cruel. It hides inside a number you have been trained your whole life to trust. The average.

You have been taught to care about your average return. Earn seven percent a year on average, the thinking goes, and the plan works. It is a reasonable belief. It is also, in retirement, dangerously incomplete, because two people can earn the exact same average and end up in completely different worlds. One retires comfortable. One runs out. Same average. Let me show you the trick.

A Magic Trick with Two Retirees

Willy B. Rich and Betty Wont both retire in the same year with the same one million dollars. Both draw the same income from it to live on. And here is the part that should stop you cold: over the next twenty-five years, both earn the exact same annual returns. Not similar. Identical. The very same list of good years and bad years. ***There is only one difference between them***: *Willy gets the good years first and the bad years last. Betty gets the same years in reverse*. Average them out and you would get the same number twice.

They do not end up in the same place. Not even close. Willy sails into his nineties with more money than he started with. Betty runs dry in her early eighties, rationing and frightened. Same million. Same withdrawals. Same returns. Different order. Opposite lives.

Betty had the bad luck to retire into a rough market. In her first few years, stocks fell hard, and because she was already retired, she was pulling money out to live the entire time they were down. Every dollar she withdrew during the slump had to be raised by selling shares at fire-sale prices. She was quietly liquidating her portfolio at precisely the wrong moment, and each of those cheap sales permanently removed shares that would never be there to recover when the market finally turned. And it did turn. But by the time the good years arrived, there was simply less of Betty's portfolio left to enjoy them.

Willy retired into calm. His good years came first. He spent the early stretch of his retirement withdrawing from a portfolio that was growing underneath him, quietly building a cushion before his own rough patch ever showed up. And when Willy's bad market finally did arrive, years later, it landed on a larger portfolio with far fewer retirement years left to damage. Same storm. It simply struck Willy's house after he had built the seawall, and it struck Betty's on the afternoon she moved in.

That is sequence of returns risk, and it is the single most counterintuitive idea in this entire book. Read the trick again if you need to, because almost nobody believes it the first time:

identical average returns, identical withdrawals, wildly different endings, decided entirely by the order.

The Day a Down Market Switches Sides

To really understand the ambush, you have to see the one thing that flips the day you retire.

For your entire working life, a falling market was your friend. When you were forty-five and still adding to your accounts, a crash was a sale. Your next paycheck bought more shares at lower prices, and you cheered, or at least you should have. Every downturn during your career was quietly making you richer, because you were a buyer, and buyers love low prices.

The day you retire, you stop being a buyer and become a seller. And on that day, with no announcement and no warning, the falling market switches sides. The very same thirty percent drop that was a gift at forty-five becomes a wound at sixty-six, because now you are not adding shares at the low, you are subtracting them to pay your grocery bill. One identical event, a market decline, is a blessing to the person putting money in and a slow bleed to the person taking money out.

Nobody rings a bell to tell you the switch has happened. You simply cross, quietly, from the side of the market that loves a crash to the side that fears it. And most people make that crossing without ever noticing the ground has changed beneath their feet.

The Retirement Red Zone

So when is the ambush most dangerous? There is a specific, identifiable window, and it is worth burning into memory. Call it the retirement red zone: roughly the five years before and the five years after the day you stop working.

Why that window? Because inside it, two dangerous things are true at the same time. Your portfolio is at its largest, the biggest it will ever be, which means a percentage loss is also the biggest dollar loss of your life. And you are either about to begin or have just begun withdrawing, which means you have the least ability to simply wait a decline out by not touching your money. A big balance, fresh withdrawals, and no time to recover. That is the red zone, and a bad market that lands inside it does damage that the very same market would barely scratch a decade later.

Here is the proof of how completely timing outweighs size. A brutal thirty percent drop in year twenty of your retirement is survivable, sometimes almost unnoticeable, because your remaining horizon is short and your withdrawals have already done most of their work. That identical thirty percent drop in year two can end the plan outright. It is not the size of the loss that decides your fate. It is the year it chooses to arrive. The market does not know or care when you retired. The ambush is simply what we call it when the market strikes near that date.

You Cannot Pick the Market, but You Can Refuse to Be Forced to Sell

Now for the good news, because there is real good news here, and it is bigger than the bad.

You cannot control the order of your returns. Whether your retirement opens with a boom or a bust is very largely luck, and no one, not me, not anyone with an honest track record, can reliably tell you in advance which one you will draw. If that were the whole story, retirement would be a coin flip, and this would be a very short and very depressing chapter.

But the order of returns is not actually what ruins people. Being forced to sell into a bad order is what ruins people. Betty did not fail because the market fell early. Betty failed because, when the market fell early, she had no choice but to sell into it. The luck was the crash. The ruin was the forced sale. And the forced sale, unlike the crash, is entirely within your power to design away.

The tool for doing it is almost embarrassingly simple, which is exactly why it works. Before you retire, you carve off two to four years of your spending and park it in something safe and stable: cash, short-term bonds, the boring instruments that do not fall when stocks do. That is your reserve. Then, when a bad market arrives, and sooner or later it will, you do not sell a single share into it. You live off the reserve and you leave your stocks completely alone to heal on their own schedule. When the good times return, you refill the reserve from the gains. That is the whole mechanism, and it quietly converts you from a forced seller at the worst imaginable moment into a patient owner who can outlast any storm.

Willy had that reserve. When his early market wobbled, he sipped from the safe money and never once touched his stocks at a low. Betty did not, so she sold. Same market, same starting million, same withdrawals. The only difference was that one of them built a seawall before the storm and the other did not. The order was luck. The seawall was a choice.

What to Do About the Ambush

Let me turn all of this into something you can act on before you close the book tonight.

First, respect the red zone. The five years on either side of your retirement date are the most financially fragile of your entire life. Not the scariest headlines, not the biggest crashes in history, these specific and ordinary-looking years. Treat them with the care they quietly deserve.

Second, build the reserve before you need it, not in the middle of the panic. Two to four years of spending, set aside in safe and stable assets, in place before you retire. A seawall is poured in the calm. No one in the history of the world has ever successfully poured concrete during the flood.

Third, in any downturn, make yourself impossible to force. Spend from the reserve. Leave the stocks alone. Refill in the good years. If you never have to sell your growth investments at a low, the ambush loses almost all of its power over you, because its power was never really the crash. It was the forced sale the crash created.

And fourth, hold on to the reframe, because it is the entire chapter compressed into a single line. The order of returns you get is luck. The order of returns that ruins you is a choice. You cannot pick the market. You can make certain it never picks your pocket.

You have now met both of the dangers that stalk the growth side of your plan. The silent thief, who works slowly across the decades and quietly shrinks what your money can buy. And the ambush, who works all at once and strikes in the fragile years around your retirement. One is patient, one is sudden, and between them they explain why so many careful, well-funded, genuinely intelligent people still lie awake worried about their own comfortable retirements.

Which raises a natural and hopeful question. Is there a single tool built to soften both at once, something that keeps you invested enough to outrun the thief while cushioning the blow if the ambush strikes early? There is. And it has quietly become one of the most improved instruments in all of retirement planning over the last decade. That is exactly where we go next.

CHAPTER FIVE

Buffered Growth: Enjoying the Upside
Without Fearing the Drop

How Registered Index-Linked Annuities Give Skeptical Investors a Seat at the Table

You have now met the two dangers that stalk the growth side of your plan. The silent thief of inflation, who quietly shrinks what your money can buy across a long retirement. And the ambush of bad timing, who strikes all at once in the fragile years around your retirement date. In the inflation chapter I made the case that equities are the only long-run remedy the historical record supports for the first. In the last chapter I showed how a simple reserve keeps the second from ever forcing your hand. Perhaps you found both arguments convincing. Or perhaps you found them convincing intellectually and not at all emotionally. If so, this chapter is for you, because it is about a single modern tool built to soften both dangers at once.

Because here is the plain truth, the one any honest advisor will admit when the door is closed: knowing something is right and being able to live with it are two very different things. You can understand, at a rational level, that a diversified equity portfolio held over twenty-five years has, in the historical record, outpaced inflation over every such period. You can accept every number. And you can still lie awake the night the market drops fifteen percent, wondering whether this is the time it all falls apart.

That is not weakness. That is humanity. And a financial plan that ignores your humanity is not a good financial plan, regardless of how mathematically elegant it might be.

So the question this chapter answers is a practical one: Is there a way to participate in the long-run growth of the equity markets, to capture enough of that inflation-fighting return, without exposing yourself to the full, unfiltered drops that make equity investing so emotionally difficult for so many people?

The answer is yes. And the vehicle that makes it possible is called a registered index-linked annuity, or RILA. It is one of the most significant and genuinely useful innovations in retirement income planning to emerge in the last decade or so. And it was built, almost precisely, for the person who read these last two chapters and thought: I understand the argument. I am just not sure I can handle the ride.

THE SCENIC DRIVE PROBLEM

Before we get into what a RILA is and how it works, I want to revisit a story, because it captures the problem we are solving better than any product description ever could.

Imagine a husband and wife setting out on one of the great American road trips to celebrate their retirement: Pennsylvania's Route 6, a journey through the Allegheny National Forest, winding through 19 state parks and forests, past covered bridges and small towns and vistas that unfold around every bend.

They set out with a full tank. But early in the trip, they pass a sign: "Last gas station for 100 miles." The wife glances at her husband. "Sweetheart, we should stop for gas." He checks the gauge, 120 miles left, and waves it off. "We're fine."

A little farther along: "Next gas station: 80 miles." Her eyebrows go up. He checks again. "Ninety-five miles left. No need to worry."

Then 50 miles to the next station. Then 20. He is always just ahead of the math, always reassuring her, always watching the gauge. They make it, rolling in with 8 miles to spare. He smiles. "See? I told you we were fine."

At the resort, the receptionist greets them warmly. "You came in on Route 6, didn't you? Both AAA and National Geographic rate it one of the most spectacular scenic drives in America. Wasn't it just breathtaking?" The couple exchanges a look. They hadn't seen the rolling hills. They hadn't noticed the golden light filtering through the trees. They hadn't taken in the small towns, the covered bridges, the vistas. They had spent the entire drive watching the gauge.

A sound retirement plan gives you the confidence to watch the scenery, not the gauge.

The Two Faces of Gas Gauge Retirement

Over the years, I have learned that gas gauge retirement is not one condition. It is two. They look nothing alike from the outside. Underneath, they are exactly the same disease.

The first face belongs to a couple we will call Buck and Penny Pincher. Buck and Penny did everything right. They saved for forty years. They paid off the house. Their accounts hold more money than they ever imagined having. And they have not enjoyed a single dollar of it.

Buck and Penny eat dinner at 4:15, because the early bird senior special ends at 5:00, and heaven forbid they pay full price for the same piece of salmon that costs four dollars less if you order it while the sun is still high. Penny reads every menu from right to left, prices first, food second. Their idea of a vacation is a day trip to see Penny's sister, two exits up the turnpike, with sandwiches packed in a cooler so they do not have to stop anywhere that charges money. They have talked about the Alaska cruise for fifteen years. It is always going to happen next year. It is never going to happen. Ask them why, and they will tell you they are being careful. But careful is not the right word. The right word is frightened. Somewhere along the way, the habit of saving hardened into a fear of spending, and now they sit atop a fortune they cannot give themselves permission to touch. They have a full tank. They refuse to burn a drop of fuel.

The second face belongs to a retiree we will call Al Nighter. Al is the opposite of Buck and Penny in every visible way. Al spends. Al travels. Al bought the boat. But Al has a different problem: Al cannot look away from the gauge.

Al retired three years ago, and he has never worked harder in his life, as the unpaid, full-time, self-appointed surveillance officer of his own portfolio. The financial news is on at breakfast. His phone buzzes with price alerts through lunch. He checks the futures markets at eleven o'clock at night, standing in the kitchen in his bathrobe, because he cannot go to bed until he knows what happened to bitcoin today. Al does not own any bitcoin. It does not matter. If bitcoin fell, something is wrong with the world, and Al needs to know about it. His grandson hit a double last Saturday, and Al missed it, because Al was in the bleachers looking down at a red number on a small screen. Al has the fuel. Al is spending the fuel. And Al has not seen one mile of scenery since the day he retired, because his eyes have never once left the dashboard. He earned his name honestly: every night is an all-nighter when you cannot go to sleep until the foreign markets open.

Buck and Penny are afraid to burn the fuel. Al cannot stop staring at the gauge. Two completely different behaviors, one couple who will not spend, one man who will not look up, and yet it is the same condition, with the same root cause: a retirement plan that accumulated money but never converted that money into confidence. Nobody ever showed them a structure that would let them stop worrying. So they never stopped.

That is the problem we are solving. Not the mathematical problem of whether stocks outperform bonds over twenty-five years, which we settled a couple of chapters ago. The human problem of whether you can actually enjoy your retirement while your money is invested in a way that requires you to tolerate real volatility along the way.

An investor who spends their entire retirement watching the market, anxiously checking their balance, dreading the next correction, lying awake after a bad week, is Al Nighter. An investor who cannot bring themselves to enjoy what they have built, who defers every pleasure to a next year that never arrives, is Buck and Penny. Both have technically made sound financial decisions. Both are living the wrong retirement. They have the fuel. They cannot enjoy the drive.

What if there were a way to structure part of your portfolio so that the gauge, the market level, simply stopped being something you needed to watch with anxiety? What if you could participate meaningfully in the market's growth, while knowing with certainty that your downside in any given period was limited to a defined, pre-agreed amount?

That is precisely what a Registered Index Linked Annuity provides.

WHAT IS A REGISTERED INDEX LINKED ANNUITY?

Let us start with plain language, because this product is often described in a way that is needlessly complicated.

A Registered Index Linked Annuity is a contract between you and an insurance company. You deposit a sum of money for a defined period, typically one, three, or six years. During that period, your account can grow based on the performance of a market index, most commonly the S&P 500, though other indices are available. And if the market falls during that period, your loss is limited. You will not lose everything. You will not lose most of it. You will lose only up to a pre-defined amount, which you agree to in advance.

That pre-defined limit is called a buffer. Think of it as a financial shock absorber built into your contract.

In exchange for that buffer, you give something up on the upside. Your gains in any given period are typically subject to a cap, a maximum return you can earn, regardless of how well the index performs. If the market rises 30 percent but your cap is 11 percent, you earn 11 percent. You do not participate in the full gain above your cap.

That is the fundamental trade-off: you give up some upside in exchange for a defined downside buffer. And for the investor who has been sitting on the sidelines, watching inflation erode their purchasing power, unable to bring themselves to accept the full volatility of the equity market, that trade-off is not a sacrifice. It is a lifeline.

KEY TERMS: Understanding Your RILA

Buffer

The percentage of loss the insurance company absorbs before you experience any loss. A 10% buffer means the market must fall more than 10% before you lose a single dollar. The first 10% of any decline is absorbed by the insurer.

Cap

The maximum return you can earn in a given contract period, regardless of how much higher the index rises. If your cap is 11% and the market rises 25%, you earn 11%. The cap is the price of your buffer.

Participation Rate

Some RILAs use a participation rate instead of or in addition to a cap. A 70% participation rate means you earn 70 cents of every dollar the index gains, with no hard ceiling. Higher buffers typically come with lower participation rates.

Contract Term

The defined period over which your buffer and cap apply, typically one, three, or six years. At the end of each term, gains (up to the cap) are locked in and a new term begins.

THE TWO INVESTORS: A HYPOTHETICAL ILLUSTRATION

Abstract descriptions only go so far. Let us look at a concrete hypothetical that shows what this buffer actually means in practice across a realistic market environment.

The following illustration uses 25 years of actual S&P 500 index returns from 2000 through 2024, one of the most turbulent and instructive periods in modern market history. It includes the dot-com crash, the September 11 attacks, the 2008 financial crisis, the COVID collapse of 2020, and the inflation-driven downturn of 2022. In other words, it includes the full force of everything the market can throw at a retiree.

We compare two hypothetical investors, each starting with $100,000. One investor participates in the full index, the raw S&P 500 total return, with no buffer and no ceiling. The other participates in a hypothetical RILA-style strategy: an 11 percent annual growth cap, with a 0 percent floor, meaning they never experience a negative year, regardless of how far the market falls.

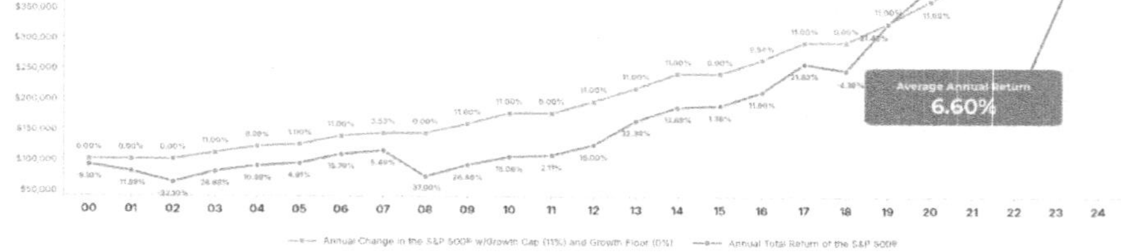

Figure 5.1: Hypothetical comparison of $100,000 invested in the S&P 500 Total Return (red) vs. a hypothetical strategy with an 11% annual cap and 0% floor (green), 2000-2024. Past performance is not indicative of future results. This illustration is hypothetical and for educational purposes only.

The results are striking, and the chart makes the story visual in a way that words alone cannot.

The full-market investor, the red line, experiences the full ride. They watch their $100,000 plunge nearly 40 percent in the dot-com bust. They see it partially recover, then collapse again by more than 37 percent in 2008. They endure 2022's sharp decline. But they also capture every up year in full, the 28 percent gains, the 32 percent gains, the 25 percent surge in 2024. Over 25 years, they average 7.70 percent per year.

The buffered investor, the green line, has a completely different experience. In the years the market falls, they simply earn zero. Not a loss, zero. Their balance does not decline. In 2001 and 2002, when the market lost nearly 40 percent over two years, they lost nothing. In 2008, when the market fell 37 percent in a single year, they lost nothing. In 2022, they lost nothing. They earn zero in the bad years and up to 11 percent in the good years, capped, but still growing.

Over 25 years, the buffered investor averages 6.60 percent per year. They end with meaningfully less than the full-market investor, but they got there on a dramatically smoother road, without a single year of loss, and without a single year in which a market collapse erased years of growth.

S&P 500 Total Return (No Buffer)	Hypothetical RILA Strategy (11% Cap / 0% Floor)
Average Annual Return: 7.70%	Average Annual Return: 6.60%
Worst Single Year: -37.00% (2008)	Worst Single Year: 0.00%

Years with Losses: 6 of 25	Years with Losses: 0 of 25
Deepest Drawdown: ~50%	Deepest Drawdown: 0%
Ending Value: ~$620,000	Ending Value: ~$490,000
Emotional Experience: Significant anxiety	Emotional Experience: Manageable confidence

This illustration is hypothetical, for educational purposes only, and does not represent the performance of any specific product or security. Actual RILA products vary significantly in their terms, caps, buffers, fees, and features. Past performance of the S&P 500 is not indicative of future results. Data source: Yahoo Finance GSPC Historical Prices, accessed 01/10/25. It is not possible to invest directly in an index. Standard & Poor's, S&P, and S&P 500 are registered trademarks of Standard & Poor's Financial Services LLC. Please consult a qualified financial professional before making any investment decision.

The difference in ending value, roughly $130,000 over 25 years, represents the cost of the buffer. That is a real cost, and it should not be minimized. But consider what you received for it: not a single year of loss over a 25-year period that included three of the worst market environments in modern history. Not a single moment when you were forced to watch your retirement savings decline. Not a single year when the anxiety of the market made you question whether you should sell and move to cash, the single most damaging decision a long-run investor can make.

For many investors, that cost is not just acceptable. It is the precise price of being able to stay invested at all. And history suggests that an investor who remains invested through a full market cycle is likely to be far better positioned than an investor who flees to cash during the first major correction, which is exactly what unbuffered equity exposure has led a significant percentage of investors to do.

> ***A slightly lower return that you can actually live with will always beat a higher return that you cannot.***

> *Be sure to read the story of Willy B. Rich and Betty Wont's friends, Constance Gaines and Upson Downs, in* ***Appendix B****. They prove the same point from a different angle: that a higher average return can still lose to a steadier lower one, once withdrawals enter the picture.*

WHO IS THIS PRODUCT FOR?

Let me be honest with you: a registered index-linked annuity is not the right tool for every investor. No single product is. Understanding who benefits most from this structure is every bit as important as understanding how the structure works.

The RILA May Be Right For You If:

- You understand intellectually that equities are necessary to outpace inflation over the long run, but you cannot tolerate the full volatility of the open market.
- You have watched previous market declines and made, or came very close to making, the decision to sell and move to safety. That instinct, acted upon, is precisely what a RILA is built to prevent.
- You are in or near retirement and cannot afford a significant multi-year drawdown in the early years of your distribution phase, when sequence-of-returns risk is at its most dangerous.
- You want meaningful growth potential, not just the 2 to 3 percent real return of bonds and CDs, but you want that growth within a defined and predictable risk envelope.

CDs are FDIC insured to specific limits and offer a fixed rate of return if held to maturity, whereas investing in securities is subject to market risk including loss of principal.

- You value the ability to know, before each contract period begins, exactly what your worst-case outcome is. That predictability has genuine value that does not show up in any rate-of-return calculation.

The RILA May Not Be the Right Fit If:

- You have a long investment horizon, 20 or more years, and the genuine *emotional* capacity to hold through market downturns without selling. In that case, uncapped equity exposure will likely produce stronger long-run results.
- You need complete liquidity. RILAs are insurance contracts with defined terms and potential surrender charges during the contract period. They are not appropriate for money you may need to access on short notice.
- You are seeking guaranteed income you cannot outlive. Although some RILAs have income riders available, a RILA is really a growth vehicle, not an income vehicle. If your primary need is a guaranteed income stream, other products, including income annuities, may be more appropriate.

THE BEHAVIORAL FINANCE CASE FOR BUFFERED GROWTH

Earlier, in the inflation chapter, we spent real time on the psychology of investing: loss aversion, the savanna problem, the damage done by checking your statements too often. We introduced those ideas to explain why people make poor investment decisions even when they know better.

Here is the practical punchline of all that behavioral science: a financial product that reduces the psychological cost of staying invested is not just emotionally comfortable. It is financially superior to a theoretically optimal product that the investor cannot hold.

This is a point that gets lost in many investment discussions, because the math is always done on paper. On paper, uncapped equity exposure wins over 25 years. But that calculation assumes the investor actually holds their equity portfolio through every correction, every crisis, every frightening headline, every year when their statements arrive and show a number significantly lower than the one from 12 months ago.

In practice, many investors do not hold. They sell. They move to cash. They wait for things to "calm down." And by the time things calm down, they have missed the recovery, which, in almost every case in market history, happens faster and more dramatically than anyone expected.

The academic term for this gap between the return of an investment and the return actually earned by investors in that investment is called ***the behavior gap.*** It has been studied extensively by researchers including Carl Richards, Dalbar, and others, and the findings are sobering: the average equity investor consistently earns significantly less than the average equity fund, because they buy high and sell low, driven by exactly the fear and loss aversion we described in the previous chapter.

~1.5%

The estimated annual return lost by average equity investors due to fear-driven buying and selling decisions, the "behavior gap." A buffered structure that keeps investors in the market can more than offset its cost in caps and fees. (Source: Dalbar QAIB Report)

A RILA does not eliminate the behavior gap by improving investor psychology. It eliminates it by removing the trigger.

When you know your downside in any given year is zero, or some defined, limited amount, the panic that drives poor decisions simply has less ammunition. The gauge stops being something you watch with dread. The drive becomes something you can actually enjoy.

HOW RILAS FIT INTO A WEALTHCARE PORTFOLIO

A Registered Index Linked Annuity is not a replacement for a diversified investment portfolio. It is a component of one, specifically, the component that serves investors who need equity-linked growth but require a defined buffer structure to stay the course.

There is no guarantee that a diversified portfolio will enhance overall returns or outperform a non-diversified portfolio. Diversification does not protect against market risk.

In the integrated Wealthcare framework at the heart of this book, we think about your retirement assets in three distinct layers, or buckets, each with a different job to do: Safety, Income, and Growth.

Layer	Purpose	Typical Vehicles	Time Horizon
Liquidity Reserve	Fund 2-4 years of living expenses without touching growth assets	Cash, money market, short-term bonds	Immediate
Buffered Growth	Provide equity-linked returns	RILAs, structured products	3-7 years

	within a defined risk envelope for investors who need the guardrails to stay invested		
Long-Term Growth	Generate the inflation-beating real returns that sustain purchasing power across a full retirement	Diversified equity portfolios, dividend stocks, global index funds	10+ years

The Buffered Growth layer is where a RILA lives. It is not the liquidity layer, it is not designed for money you need next month. And it is not the long-term growth layer, it will not deliver the uncapped compound returns of a fully invested equity portfolio over 25 years. It sits between those two layers, doing a specific job: capturing meaningful market participation with a defined floor, for investors who need that structure to remain committed to growth at all.

Asset allocation does not ensure a profit or protect against a loss.

For a great many people, particularly those who worked hard and long for what they have accumulated and are acutely aware of what it would mean to lose a meaningful piece of it, the Buffered Growth layer is not optional. It is the very thing that makes the rest of the plan emotionally survivable. And a plan that is emotionally survivable is a plan that actually gets carried out, rather than abandoned at the first sign of trouble.

WHAT TO ASK BEFORE YOU INVEST

RILAs are insurance products, and like all insurance products, the details matter enormously. The category is sound. Individual contracts vary widely. Here are the questions every investor should have answered before committing to any RILA contract:

- What is the buffer, and what index does it apply to? A 10 percent buffer on the S&P 500 means something very different from a 10 percent buffer on a more volatile index.
- What is the cap, and how is it set? Caps change at each contract renewal. Understand what drives cap levels and what your options are if caps decline significantly at renewal.
- What are the surrender charges, and for how long do they apply? Most RILAs have surrender charge periods during which early withdrawal carries a penalty. Know exactly what those terms are before you commit.
- Is there a fee embedded in the product, and how does it affect your net return? Some RILAs are fee-based; others build their cost into the spread between the index return and your cap. Understand what you are paying, in total.
- What is the financial strength rating of the issuing insurance company? The buffer and cap guarantees are backed by the insurer's claims-paying ability. Credit quality matters.
- What happens at the end of each contract term? Understand your renewal options, including the ability to adjust allocations, change terms, or exit without penalty at term end.

THE BIGGER PICTURE: THE BUFFER AS A GATEWAY, NOT A DESTINATION

I want to close this chapter with a perspective that is too often missing from discussions of buffered investment products.

A Registered Index Linked Annuity is not the destination. It is the gateway.

The destination, the goal of a well-constructed retirement plan, is a portfolio that generates sufficient real return to sustain your purchasing power across a retirement that may last 25 or 30 years, while providing enough stability that you can actually enjoy the journey rather than spending every day watching the gauge.

For some investors, a fully invested equity portfolio with proper liquidity reserves is the right structure to get to that destination. Their temperament, their experience, their financial security, their other income sources, pension, Social Security, rental income, give them the buffer they need to tolerate equity volatility without flinching.

For other investors, and I believe this is a far larger group than the financial planning profession typically admits, the emotional cost of full equity exposure is simply too high. Not because they are unsophisticated. Not because they do not understand the data. But because they are human beings, with real memories of real losses, real responsibilities, and a real desire to enjoy the retirement they worked so hard to reach.

For those investors, a RILA is not a concession to fear. It is a rational, thoughtful, evidence-informed response to the reality of who they are and how they experience financial risk. It is the structure that lets them participate in market growth, that keeps them in the game, earning real returns, outpacing inflation, when the alternative would be flight to the false safety of cash and bonds.

And in our hypothetical illustration, the investor who stayed invested for 25 years, earning an average of 6.60 percent per year with zero down years, accomplished something meaningful for their financial security and their legacy. They did not do quite as well as the investor who held a fully invested equity portfolio without flinching. But they did far better than the investor who fled to cash the first time the market dropped 20 percent, which, without the buffer that a RILA provides, is exactly what a meaningful percentage of investors have historically done.

"The best investment strategy is not the one with the highest theoretical return. It is the one you can actually live with, for 25 years, through everything the market will throw at you."

CONCLUSION: THE DRIVE IS THE POINT

Remember the couple on Route 6. They had the fuel. They made it to the resort. By any objective measure, the trip was a success. But they spent the entire drive watching the gauge, and they missed everything that made the trip worth taking.

Retirement is the drive. The financial plan is the fuel. And a good financial plan does not just get you there, it lets you actually look out the window along the way.

A Registered Index Linked Annuity is not a magic solution. It is a trade-off, chosen deliberately, by an investor who has decided that the confidence that comes with a defined buffer is worth more to them than the additional return they might theoretically capture without it. For the right investor, in the right portion of the right portfolio, it is one of the most elegant trade-offs available in modern retirement planning.

In the chapters ahead, we will keep building the complete Wealthcare framework, turning to the remaining dangers of a long life, the rising cost of care, the tax bill that swells with every year, and the survivor who is left to face it all, and to the integrated approach that ties every piece of the plan together into something coherent, durable, and genuinely yours.

For now, consider this: the goal was never just to have enough money. The goal was always to enjoy the drive.

Important Disclosures

Registered Index Linked Annuities (RILAs) are insurance products issued by insurance companies and are not FDIC insured, not bank guaranteed, and may lose value. RILAs involve investment risk, including possible loss of principal beyond any applicable buffer. All guarantees are backed by the claims-paying ability of the issuing insurance company.

The hypothetical illustration in this chapter is for educational purposes only and does not represent the performance of any specific product, investment, or account. Actual results will vary. Past performance of the S&P 500 Index is not indicative of future results. It is not possible to invest directly in an index.

Caps, buffers, and participation rates referenced in this chapter are illustrative only and are subject to change at each contract renewal. Actual product terms vary by issuer, contract, and market conditions at the time of issue.

This chapter is adapted from the forthcoming book The Longevity Trap, by George McReynolds, CFP(r) | McReynolds & Company, LLC | Wealthcare Legacy Management(tm). This material is provided for informational and educational purposes only and does not constitute investment, tax, or legal advice. Please consult a qualified financial professional regarding your individual situation.

CHAPTER SIX

The Long Storm

We have spent three chapters on your money and how to grow it, shield it, and keep yourself from panicking out of it. The silent thief, the ambush, and the tool built to soften them both. That is the growth side of a long life handled.

Now we turn to the danger that most people handle by pretending it does not exist.

It is the third of the five forces that make your retirement different from the average person's, and it is the one you least want to read about, which is exactly why it is the one most likely to hurt you. It is the long, slow, expensive possibility that at some point in a long life, you will need someone to help you live it. I call it the long storm, because unlike the ambush, it does not strike and then leave. It settles in, and it can stay for years.

The Blank Space in Every Plan

Open almost any comfortable person's retirement plan and you will find, somewhere near the back, a blank space where long-term care should be. It is rarely a decision. It is an avoidance. The subject is unpleasant, the odds feel abstract, and so the line simply never gets filled in.

The affluent are the worst offenders, and they have a favorite phrase for it. I'll die with my golf shoes on. They picture themselves dropping cleanly on the golf course at ninety-two, mid-backswing, having never once troubled a nurse.

It is a lovely fantasy, and I hope it comes true for you. But hope is not a plan, and the arithmetic points hard the other way.

Here is the cruel twist, and it is the same twist that runs through this entire book. Remember from the first chapter that the healthy, successful, well-doctored people, the people reading this, are the ones who live the longest. Now connect that fact to this chapter. The longer you live, the higher the odds that you will need care, and the longer that care is likely to last. The very longevity we have been celebrating is what loads this particular risk. The person most certain they will never need care is, statistically, among the most likely to need it, because they are the most likely to live long enough to get there.

The ***die with your golf-shoes-on*** crowd is not wrong to want that ending. They are wrong to bet the estate on it.

The Long Tail

Let me give you the shape of the risk, briefly, because the numbers genuinely matter here.

According to the U.S. Department of Health and Human Services, a person turning sixty-five today runs nearly a seventy percent chance of needing some form of long-term care in the years ahead.

Seventy percent! That is not a tail risk you can wave off. It is closer to the base case.

And it is expensive in a way that can truly threaten a well-built plan. In most of the country, a private room in a nursing home now runs well past a hundred thousand dollars a year. Assisted living and full-time home care cost less but are still substantial, and none of it is a one-time bill. That is the part the gentle little word care manages to hide. Care is not an event. It is a duration. The average need runs around three years, but a meaningful share stretch well beyond five, and a cognitive decline like dementia can mean the better part of a decade. That is why I call it the long tail: not the average length, but the real possibility of a very long one, arriving at the exact age you are most likely to reach.

The Point Is to Stay Out of One

Now let me say something that reshapes how you should think about this entire chapter, because it is the part almost everyone gets exactly backward. *The purpose of planning for care is not to fund a comfortable stay in a nursing home. It is to keep you out of one.* A nursing home is, for the most part, where people end up when there was no plan and no better option left. A good plan aims in the opposite direction, at keeping you in your own home, in your own chair, for as long as humanly possible. And here is the quiet gift buried in that: *the goal you would want anyway turns out to be the cheaper one, the healthier one, and very likely the longer one.*

Begin with what people actually want, because it is nearly unanimous. In AARP's national surveys, right around seventy-seven percent of adults over fifty say they want to remain in their own homes as they age, a figure that has barely moved in more than a decade. Almost no one dreams of the facility. And staying home is usually the far less expensive path as well. A home aide runs a national median in the neighborhood of eighty thousand dollars a year, while a private room in a nursing home now runs well past a hundred and twenty-five thousand. As long as you need help for part of the day rather than around the clock, care under your own roof costs a fraction of care in a facility.

And the money is the smallest part of it, because people simply do better at home. A 2023 review of the economic research found that home care delivered outcomes at least as good as institutional care while costing less. That should surprise no one, because home is where the things that keep a person well actually live: your own bed, your own routines, your family close by, and a reason to get out of that bed in the morning. Isolation is the opposite, and it is not merely sad. *The Centers for Disease Control now rank loneliness and social isolation alongside smoking as a serious risk to both health and length of life*, and few things isolate a person faster than being moved out of their home and away from everyone they know. Keeping you home is not the soft, sentimental choice. *On cost, on quality of life, and very likely on the sheer number of years, it is the smart one.*

So hold this thought as we turn, in a moment, to how you actually pay for care. *The pool of money we are about to build is* ***not a nursing-home fund****. It is a* ***stay-at-home fund***. It is what lets you bring the help to you, on your own terms and under your own roof, and hold the facility in reserve for only the most extreme case, if that day ever comes at all. The best-funded plan of all is the one that quietly keeps you out of the one place everyone dreads.

Do the multiplication in your head. Six figures a year, for a span measured not in months but in years, landing late in a long life.

That is not a dent in a retirement plan. For most families, it is the single largest threat to the entire estate.

And here is what makes it worse than a number on a page. A long care event rarely stops at the person receiving the care. It reaches clear across the kitchen table. It can drain the very assets meant to fund a thirty-five-year retirement, at the worst possible time. It can consume the legacy you meant to leave. And most painfully of all, it can impoverish the healthy spouse, the one who does not need a day of care, leaving them to fund whatever years remain out of whatever the storm left behind. We will give that survivor a chapter of their own before we are done. For now, simply understand that the cost of care is never really one person's cost. It is the whole household's.

Three Ways to Face the Storm

So what do you do about a risk that is likely, expensive, and open-ended? You have three honest choices, and it is worth being clear-eyed about each.

The first is to self-fund. Simply plan to pay for care out of your own assets if it comes. For the genuinely wealthy, this can work, but it carries a hidden cost that Buck and Penny would recognize in an instant. To self-fund an open-ended, six-figure-a-year risk, you have to keep a large pile of money in reserve, just in case, for decades. That money sits there, half invested and half enjoyed, quietly doing nothing but waiting for a storm that may never come. And if the storm does come and stays long enough, even a large reserve can be emptied. Self-insuring the catastrophic and open-ended is precisely the thing insurance was invented to spare you from.

The second choice is traditional long-term care insurance, and I will be honest about it, because it has earned some of its bad name. The old model had two real flaws. It was use it or lose it: pay premiums faithfully for thirty years, never need care, and every dollar was simply gone. And the industry badly underpriced these policies for years, then came back to policyholders with steep premium increases that arrived, cruelly, right around the age people could least absorb them. A great many good people dropped good coverage after a rate shock they never saw coming. Traditional coverage still has its place, but that history is real, and it soured a whole generation on the entire idea.

The third choice is the one that has quietly gotten very good over the last several years, and it is the second of the two modern innovations I promised you back in the inflation chapter. To explain it, I want to borrow a two-hundred-year-old idea from the most practical man in American history.

Ben Franklin's Lightning Rod

Take a good look at an old farmhouse in a summer thunderstorm. Look along the roofline, and you will often see a thin copper spike, with a wire running down the side of the house and into the ground. Benjamin Franklin gave us that.

Most people remember Franklin for the hundred-dollar bill, or the kite in the storm. But the thing he invented that quietly protected more homes and more families than almost anything else in his lifetime was that simple rod and wire. Franklin looked at the single most catastrophic risk to a colonial home, a lightning strike that could burn everything to the ground in a single evening, and he did something clever. He did not try to stop the storm. You cannot stop a storm. Instead, with a small, purposeful piece of copper, he gave the strike a safe path around everything that mattered, directing all of that destructive energy harmlessly into the earth.

That is exactly what modern hybrid long-term care coverage does with the financial lightning of a care event. You cannot prevent the storm of aging. But you can install a rod. With a small, deliberate portion of your wealth, you create a defined path for the catastrophic cost to travel: around your portfolio, around your legacy, and around your spouse, rather than straight through all three.

Here is how the rod actually works, in plain language. You reposition a portion of your net worth, in a single deposit, into a policy that does something a bank account simply cannot. It immediately multiplies that deposit several times over into a pool of money that is available, income-tax-free under current law, to pay for your care. Reposition roughly a hundred and fifty thousand dollars, for instance, and you might see a care pool of well over four hundred thousand available from day one, and growing larger every year after that. It could be seven hundred to eight hundred thousand dollars when you are most likely to use it at age 80 or 85.

And now the part that cures the old use it or lose it curse, the very flaw that soured everyone on traditional coverage. If you never need a single day of care, the money is not gone. *Your full premium passes to your heirs as a death benefit*, income-tax-free under current law. Read that again, because it is the whole point. The dollars you place into the rod cannot be wasted. They are not spent on insurance you might never use. They are simply repositioned, and they are now certain to do one of exactly two jobs: pay for your care if the storm comes, or pass to your family if it does not. Heads, your care is covered. Tails, your children are. There is no third outcome in which the money just disappears, and that vanishing third outcome is precisely what made people hate the old policies.

The efficiency of this can be striking. In the illustrations I have run, the internal rate of return on the care benefit has landed in the high single digits, with a tax-equivalent yield in the low double digits, numbers that compare favorably to what people expect from places carrying far more risk. The leverage tends to be even greater for men, for actuarial reasons. These figures are illustrative, and every contract is different, but the shape of the thing is remarkably consistent: a small, purposeful placement of copper, quietly redirecting a strike that would otherwise take the whole house.

Who the Lightening Rod Is For

As with the buffered growth tool in the last chapter, this is not right for everyone, and I would far rather tell you plainly than sell you loosely.

A hybrid care strategy tends to fit if you already have assets you are quietly earmarking just in case for care, money that is sitting idle against exactly this risk. It fits if safeguarding your spouse and your legacy from a long care event genuinely matters to you. It fits if the old *use it or lose it* structure is what always stopped you, because this structure removes it entirely. And it fits if you value knowing, today, exactly what your worst case looks like.

It tends not to fit if you have little in the way of liquid assets to reposition. It does not fit if you would need that money back on short notice, since these are insurance contracts with defined terms. And it honestly does not fit if you are wealthy enough to absorb an open-ended, multi-year, six-figure event without straining either your plan or your spouse, in which case you may simply choose to self-fund with your eyes wide open. There is no shame in any of these answers. *There is only shame in leaving the space blank and calling it a plan.*

What to Do About the Storm

Here is what to do, and most of it you can begin this week.

First, fill in the blank space. Every real plan has a line for care. Decide, on purpose, how yours will be funded. The one unacceptable answer is the one most people quietly choose, which is no answer at all.

Second, remember which end of the odds you are standing on. You are not the person least likely to need care. As a healthy, long-living reader of this book, you are among the most likely, because you are the most likely to live long enough to get there. Plan from that fact, not from the boots-on fantasy.

Third, if you have money sitting idle just in case, look hard at repositioning it into a rod. Turning dead money into coverage that either pays for your care or passes to your family, and cannot be wasted, is one of the most efficient moves available to a long-lived retiree.

Fourth, and this one has a clock on it, *act while you are healthy.* You cannot install a lightning rod once the storm is already overhead. This coverage has to be arranged while you are still insurable, which means the right time to look at it is well before the day you think you need it.

And fifth, do it for the person who will not need care every bit as much as for the one who might. The deepest gift of handling this risk is that it safeguards the spouse left standing, and we will come to that survivor before this book is done.

The long storm handled, we turn now to a very different kind of adversary. Not one who arrives all at once like the ambush, or settles in for years like the storm, but one who has been sitting quietly inside your largest accounts for decades, patient as a landlord, simply waiting for the day the rent finally comes due. It is time to talk about taxes.

A note on the specifics. The figures in this chapter are illustrative and for educational purposes only. They do not represent any specific product, and actual terms, multiples, growth rates, fees, and features vary significantly by contract, by issuer, and by your age and health at the time of application. Hybrid long-term care and life insurance products are insurance contracts; any guarantees are backed by the claims-paying ability of the issuing insurance company, and these products are not FDIC insured, are not bank guaranteed, and may involve surrender charges during the contract period.

Nothing in this chapter constitutes investment, tax, or legal advice. Please review any such strategy with a qualified financial professional in light of your own situation.

CHAPTER SEVEN

The Long Fuse

At the end of the last chapter I called this next adversary a landlord, patient and quiet, waiting for the rent to come due. That was generous of me. A landlord, at least, tells you the rent up front.

The truth is closer to something with a fuse on it. Because the bill you are about to meet does not sit still and wait. It grows. The longer you live, the larger it gets, and the later it detonates, which makes it the perfect fourth jaw for a book about living a long time. Time is the multiplier here too, and nowhere in your entire plan does it multiply more quietly, or more expensively, than in the very accounts you were proudest to fill.

I am talking, of course, about taxes. And specifically about the tax buried inside your largest retirement accounts, the traditional 401(k) and the traditional IRA, where the fuse has been burning, unnoticed, since the day you made your very first contribution.

"The difference between death and taxes?

Death ain't getting any worse!"

UNCLE JOE

The Partner You Never Chose

Here is a fact about your traditional retirement accounts that almost nobody feels in their bones, even though they know it perfectly well on paper.

You do not own all of that money.

When you put money into a traditional 401(k) or IRA, the government let you skip the tax on the way in. That felt like a gift, and for decades it felt like your balance was entirely yours, growing and compounding, a number that was reliably, satisfyingly large. But you never actually skipped that tax. You deferred it. Every dollar in there, the contributions and every dollar of growth stacked on top of them, will be taxed as ordinary income on the way out. Which means you have a silent partner in that account, and that partner is the IRS. They own a slice of every statement you have ever celebrated. You simply have not been sent the bill yet.

And here is the part that makes it a fuse rather than a flat bill. Their slice grows right along with yours. As your account compounds across a long retirement, the government's share compounds too. You are not merely growing your money. You are growing their money, tax-deferred, on your dime, until the day they decide to collect.

Why a Long Life Lights the Fuse

So when do they collect? On their schedule, not yours. It is called a required minimum distribution, an RMD, and it is exactly what it sounds like. Starting at age seventy-three today, and rising to seventy-five by 2033, the government requires you to begin pulling money out of these accounts every single year, whether you need it or not, and to pay ordinary income tax on every dollar you pull.

Now watch what a long life does to this, because this is the whole chapter in one motion.

First, the longer you live, the longer your account compounds before those forced withdrawals even begin, which means the bomb is simply bigger by the time the fuse reaches it. Second, the required withdrawal is a percentage of the account, and that percentage climbs every year you age. It begins modestly, around four percent at seventy-three. By eighty it is closer to five. By eighty-five it is past six. By ninety it is more than eight, and it keeps rising from there. So the deeper into a long life you travel, the larger your balance and the larger the slice you are forced to pull from it, both at the same time.

Put those two together and you arrive at one of the strangest and most infuriating facts in all of retirement. A long-lived, disciplined saver can find themselves, in their eighties, paying tax in a higher bracket than they ever paid during their working years. Read that again. The reward for a lifetime of careful saving and a long, healthy life can be the highest tax rates of your entire life, arriving in your ninth decade, on money you may not even need to spend. The longer the fuse burns, the bigger the blast.

The Stealth Taxes

And the ordinary income tax is only the detonator. It sets off a whole chain of secondary charges that most retirees never see coming, because they do not look like taxes at all. They wear polite, bureaucratic names. I call them the stealth taxes, and a long life hands every one of them more time and more income to work with.

The first is aimed straight at your Medicare. It is called IRMAA, and when your income crosses certain thresholds, your Medicare premiums simply jump, sometimes sharply. It is a cliff, not a gentle ramp: one dollar over the line and the full surcharge lands on you. Worse, it is calculated on your income from two years earlier, so a large RMD or a poorly timed conversion at seventy-three can quietly spike your Medicare premiums at seventy-five, long after you have forgotten what triggered it. IRMAA and income taxes could actually cost more than 100% of your withdrawal.

The second goes after your Social Security. As your other income rises, more and more of your Social Security benefit becomes taxable, until as much as eighty five percent of a benefit you already paid for once gets taxed all over again. You could be in the 22% marginal tax bracket and pay 40% of your withdrawal on income taxes.

And these things stack. A little more income can push you over an IRMAA cliff, drag more of your Social Security into taxation, and nudge up your bracket, all at once, so that one modest extra withdrawal ends up costing you far more than it gave you. This is the quiet machinery that turns a simple long life into a genuinely complicated tax problem.

There are potentially 85 more "tripwires" for stealth taxes when you include phase-outs, phase-ins, cliffs, surtaxes, and benefit reductions.

I am giving you the shape of these here, not the full anatomy, because the full anatomy is an entire book, and as it happens, I wrote it. If this chapter is starting to make you uneasy, the detailed field manual for every one of these stealth taxes, and exactly how to dismantle them one by one, is my book *Defuse the Bomb*, written specifically for people with seven-figure tax-deferred accounts staring straight at this problem. Consider the chapter you are reading now the aerial photograph. That book is the room-by-room tour.

The Window to Cut the Fuse

Now for the good news, because a fuse, unlike a lightning strike, can be cut before it ever reaches the charge.

The single most powerful tool for defusing this bomb is the Roth conversion, and its power is almost entirely a matter of timing. A Roth conversion means voluntarily moving money out of your tax-deferred account and into a Roth account, paying the ordinary income tax on it today, so that it, and all of its future growth, become permanently free from federal income tax under current law. You are choosing to pay the partner off early, on your terms, at today's rates, rather than letting their share keep compounding for another twenty years and detonate on theirs.

And there is a specific window where this works best, one that almost nobody uses well. It is the stretch between the day you retire and the day RMDs begin, those gap years in your sixties and very early seventies when the paycheck has stopped but the forced withdrawals have not yet started. For many people, income dips during that stretch, which means you may have room to convert money at surprisingly low tax rates, deliberately filling up the lower brackets on purpose, year after year, shrinking the future bomb one controlled slice at a time.

That window is closing on two fronts at once, which is why this is urgent rather than someday. It closes for you personally the moment RMDs begin and your income jumps back up. And it may be closing for everyone, because today's tax rates are low by historical standards. We are not far removed from a time when the top federal bracket sat above ninety percent, and there is no guarantee that today's comparatively gentle rates will last. If they rise, the cost of defusing this bomb rises right along with them for everyone still holding one. The dollars you convert at today's rates may, in hindsight, turn out to have been on sale.

This is exactly the strategy Willy B. Rich used and Betty Wont did not. Willy spent his gap years quietly converting, a bracketful at a time. By his eighties his tax-deferred balance was a fraction of what it might have been, his RMDs were modest, his Medicare surcharges never once triggered, and when his wife was widowed she inherited a plan that had already been made tax-friendly. Betty left hers untouched, proud of how large the balance looked, right up until the year her RMDs, her stealth taxes, and the widow's penalty all arrived together and introduced her to the highest tax rates she had ever paid, at eighty-six, with no working income left to soften them. Same discipline. Same long life. One of them cut the fuse. The other stood back and admired the size of the bomb.

What to Do About the Fuse

Here is how to begin cutting your own fuse, and the sooner the better, because every one of these levers is worth more the earlier you pull it.

First, look at your traditional retirement balance and see it honestly, as a partnership rather than a possession. Ask yourself what it would truly be worth after the IRS takes its share, and then make your plans around that smaller, more honest number.

Second, treat your gap years as the rare opportunity they are. The stretch between retirement and RMDs is the best tax-planning window of your entire life, and it does not come back once it closes. Do not sleepwalk through it.

Third, look seriously at Roth conversions during those lower-income years, filling the lower brackets on purpose. Paying a known, modest tax today can spare you a much larger, compounding one later.

Fourth, plan the conversions around the survivor. One of the strongest reasons of all to defuse the bomb early is to spare the spouse who will one day face these very accounts alone, taxed in the cramped single brackets, with no one left to split the income.

And fifth, get real help, and get the full manual. The timing of all of this, played against your income, your Medicare, your Social Security, and the calendar, is genuinely intricate, and small mistakes here are expensive ones. Work with a tax professional who does this deliberately, and read Defuse the Bomb for the complete, step-by-step playbook. This chapter told you the bomb is real and the fuse is long. That book shows you, wire by wire, how to cut it.

We have now walked through four of the five forces that make a long retirement different from a short one. The slow thief, the sudden ambush, the long storm, and the long fuse. And you may have noticed that a particular figure has stepped quietly into three of those four chapters, always in the hardest moment, always alone. The surviving spouse. It is time, at last, to give that person the chapter they deserve.

Traditional IRA account owners have considerations to make before performing a Roth IRA conversion. These primarily include income tax consequences on the converted amount in the year of conversion, withdrawal limitations from a Roth IRA, and income limitations for future contributions to a Roth IRA. In addition, if you are required to take a required minimum distribution (RMD) in the year you convert, you must do so before converting to a Roth IRA.

This chapter is for general education only and is not tax, legal, or investment advice. Tax laws are complex, change over time, and apply differently to every individual. Roth conversions and related strategies are not appropriate for everyone and can carry significant and sometimes irreversible tax consequences. Please consult a qualified tax professional regarding your own circumstances before taking any action.

CHAPTER EIGHT

The One Who's Left

This chapter is different from the ones before it, and you may feel the change within the first few pages. The other four dangers were problems of money, and we met them with numbers and strategies and a certain amount of dark humor. This one is a problem of love, and it deserves a quieter voice.

You have noticed her already. In the chapter on the long storm, she was the healthy spouse left to fund whatever the care event did not consume. In the chapter on taxes, she was the one who inherited the accounts alone, in the single brackets, at the worst possible moment. She has been standing at the edge of nearly every danger in this book, and I have kept promising you her chapter. This is it. She is the fifth jaw, and she bites the longest of all, because she is not a risk to your money. She is the person your money was always meant to protect.

And she is not rare. There are roughly 11.8 million widows in the United States today, and by most estimates another 2,800 women join their ranks every single day. This is not an edge case to be hedged against. For a married couple, it is very nearly the ending the numbers predict. Let me introduce you to her properly. Her name is Sue Vivor, and to understand her, you first have to meet her husband.

Les and Sue

Les Prepared was a good man. I want to say that plainly, right at the start, because this is not a story about a fool. Les was diligent and devoted. He worked hard for forty years, saved carefully, and gave his wife a comfortable, worry-free life. He handled all of it. The accounts, the bills, the investments, the taxes, the decisions. Sue never had to think about money, and that was exactly how Les wanted it. He saw it as a gift to her, and for most of their marriage, it was.

If that arrangement sounds familiar, it should, because it is the norm and not the exception. When UBS surveyed thousands of married women for its *Own Your Worth* study, it found that fifty eight percent of them deferred the long-term financial decisions, the investing, the planning, the big irreversible choices, entirely to their husbands. Eighty five percent handled the day-to-day bills while their husband quietly ran the long-term plan. And only about one couple in five, twenty percent, actually made the major financial decisions together. Les and Sue were not unusual. They were a statistic waiting to happen.

Les did almost everything right. He did the one thing wrong that this chapter exists to warn you about, and it is a thing that millions of good, loving spouses do without ever once realizing it is a mistake. He took such complete care of the money that Sue never learned any of it. She did not know where the accounts were, or who their advisor was, or how the income actually worked, or which decisions had been quietly locked in years ago and could no longer be changed. She trusted Les completely, and Les was completely trustworthy, and so the entire plan lived inside one person's head.

The trouble is that the arrangement only works while both people are alive. The same body of UBS research found that roughly eight in ten women will end up managing their finances alone at some point, through divorce or, far more often, through widowhood. The very setup that felt like a gift is, statistically, a time bomb with a fuse of unknown length.

And then, as happens, Les died first. He usually does. And on that day, the gift quietly turned into a trap.

The Year Everything Doubled

Here is what descended on Sue Vivor, all at once, in the same year she was learning to sleep in a bed that had become too big.

Start with the raw arithmetic, because it is more brutal than most people realize, and it is baked directly into the system. When one spouse dies, the household's Social Security income drops by roughly a third. That is not an oversight or a penalty someone forgot to remove. It is simply how the program works.

The Widow's Penalty, in Three Numbers

Household income drops by roughly ONE-THIRD the day the smaller Social Security check stops forever.

Household needs, per Social Security's own researchers, fall by only about TWENTY PERCENT.

And at the very same time, her tax brackets narrow by roughly HALF, so the very same income is taxed more heavily too.

Read those three numbers together, because the gap between them is the entire problem: a survivor left to run a household that still costs about eighty cents on the dollar, on roughly sixty-five cents of income, taxed at a higher rate than either spouse ever paid while both were alive.

When two spouses are alive, two checks arrive. When one dies, the survivor keeps only the larger of the two, and the smaller check stops forever. Now hold that one-third income drop next to a second fact, documented by Social Security's own researchers: when a spouse dies, the household's needs, as measured by the poverty line, fall by only about twenty percent. Read those two numbers together, because the gap between them is the entire problem. Income falls by a third. The cost-of-living falls by only a fifth. The survivor is left running a household that still costs roughly eighty cents on the dollar with about sixty-five cents of income. That gap is the widow's penalty in its purest form, and some version of it is waiting inside almost every married couple's plan, whether they have ever noticed it or not.

The consequences show up exactly where you would expect. Researchers following thousands of American families through the long-running Health and Retirement Study found that among couples who would soon lose a spouse, the poverty rate was about four percent while both were alive. In the years right after the death, it jumped to around twelve percent. It roughly tripled. And here is the part that should stop you cold: the newly poor were not people who had been struggling all along. They were the very same households that had been perfectly fine, four percent fine, while both spouses were living. Widowhood did not simply find people who were already poor. It manufactured poverty out of families who were not.

The gender of it is unmistakable, too. A Stanford analysis of that same study found that widows end up with about twenty two percent less income than widowers in otherwise identical circumstances, along with a measurably higher chance of falling into poverty. When the survivor is the wife, which she overwhelmingly is, the penalty bites harder.

Then come the taxes, and they compound everything above. For their entire marriage, Les and Sue had filed jointly, which in the tax code means roomy brackets and a generous standard deduction built for two. The year after Les died, Sue filed as a single taxpayer. Almost nothing about her income had actually changed, but that same income was now being squeezed through the single brackets, which are roughly half as wide, with roughly half the standard deduction. Her income barely moved. Her tax bill leapt. This is the widow's penalty wearing its tax face, and it is exactly as unfair as it sounds: the code charges you more for the crime of being left alone.

And her pension, that steady monthly anchor, dropped too, for reasons we will return to shortly, because they were entirely avoidable. Quietly, in the background, her *Medicare grew more expensive as well*, since the income thresholds that trigger those surcharges are, like the tax brackets, cut roughly in half for a single person. So, *Sue Vivor found herself with less income, a larger tax bill on it, and higher Medicare premiums, all arriving in the same terrible year, stacked on top of the only loss that actually mattered to her.*

And she faced every piece of it, every form and every irreversible decision, while she was also, for the very first time in her life, simply trying to find the passwords. She was not alone in that, either. In the same UBS research, seventy-four percent of widows and divorcees said they discovered negative financial surprises, outdated wills, forgotten debts, tax problems they never knew existed, at the exact moment they were least equipped to handle them. Nearly three out of four. A plan that lives inside one person's head does not transfer cleanly to the other. It transfers as a series of shocks.

The Longest Widowhood

Now bring the whole book to bear on Sue's situation, because this is where the fifth jaw becomes the cruelest of them all.

First, dispense with the picture in your head. When most people imagine a widow, they picture a woman in her eighties. The data says otherwise. ***The U.S. Census Bureau puts the median age of widowhood at just under sixty, right around fifty-nine for a first marriage.***

Widowhood is not the final scene of a long retirement.

For a great many women, it arrives near the beginning of one, and then it stays.

And it stays a long time. *Here is perhaps the single most important number in this chapter, and it comes straight from the Census Bureau:* ***half of all widows over the age of sixty-five will outlive their husbands by fifteen years or more***. Fifteen years. Sit with that. Widowhood is not a season of grief you pass through on the way to the end. For half of the women who enter it, it is a second retirement, lived entirely solo, that can run a decade and a half or longer.

Everything else in this book has argued that you are likely to live a very long time. Turn that same lens on a marriage, and a hard truth appears. If you are going to live a long time, then one of you is going to spend a long time alone. And it is almost always the wife. Women outlive men by roughly five to six years on average, and they often married men a few years older to begin with, so the arithmetic points, again and again, to a woman living out a long final chapter by herself.

Which means Sue Vivor did not face the widow's penalty for a year or two. She faced it for the better part of two decades. And here the longevity trap bares its teeth one final time, because these penalties do not fade with the years. They deepen. That same Stanford study found that t*he income gap between widows and widowers, painful enough in the first year, actually widens again after the ten-year mark,* as savings, drawn down too quickly, run thin and pensions that were never built to last a second lifetime fall further behind. The Center for Retirement Research, which has tracked widows for decades, finds that their poverty rate, though it has improved over time, remains stubbornly and significantly higher than that of married women, and highest of all among those who live the longest.

Every penalty this chapter has named, the lost check, the higher taxes, the shrunken pension, did not strike once and then leave. They settled in for the long haul, exactly like everything else a long life amplifies. The longer Sue lived, the longer she paid.

The very longevity we have spent this entire book celebrating is what makes the survivor's chapter the longest and the heaviest. A short retirement barely has time to reach this danger. A long one lives inside it.

The Most Overlooked Person in Retirement

Here is what I have come to believe after many years of this work. The surviving spouse is the single most overlooked person in all of retirement planning.

And overlooked is precisely the word, because she is not unlikely. She is nearly certain. The Census Bureau's most recent detailed look at older Americans found that among people seventy-five and older who had ever married, fifty eight percent of the women had already experienced the death of a spouse, compared with just twenty eight percent of the men. Counting only those still widowed at the time of the survey, it was fifty four percent of women against twenty percent of men. Read that plainly: *more than half of married women will, if they live a normal lifespan, become widows.* This is not a tail risk to be hedged. It is the base case to be planned for.

And yet watch how almost every retirement plan gets built. It projects the couple's income and the couple's expenses, together, in one tidy line, all the way to the end. It quietly assumes that both people live, and spend, and pay taxes as a pair, right up until the plan simply stops. Almost no plan pauses to ask the most predictable question of all: what happens to the one who is left? What does the income look like, and the tax bill, and the whole arithmetic of the household, when it is one person, in the single brackets, for fifteen years?

That is a staggering omission, because we know exactly when the hardest financial decisions of a widow's life will land: in the very same window as the worst emotional blow she will ever absorb. On the Holmes and Rahe Stress Scale, the standard clinical measure of life stress, the death of a spouse ranks first. Number one. Above divorce, above job loss, above serious illness. And it is at that exact moment, when her capacity to make careful, irreversible financial decisions is at its very lowest, that the system hands her a mountain of them. It is little wonder that experienced advisors counsel a newly widowed client to postpone every major, irreversible money decision for anywhere from six months to a few years. A plan that never once ran the numbers for that person, at that moment, is not really a finished plan. It is a plan for the easy half of the story.

How Les Prepared Could Have Loved Her Better

So let me tell you what Les could have done, because every bit of it is something you can still do, and all of it is, at its heart, an act of love.

First, and above everything else, he could have brought Sue in. The single greatest gift is not a bigger account. It is a spouse who understands the plan. And the evidence that this matters is overwhelming. In that same UBS research, seventy-six percent of widows and divorcees said they wished they had been more involved in the long-term financial decisions while their spouse was still alive. More than three quarters of them, all speaking from the far side of the loss, all giving the identical piece of advice. And the payoff of heeding it is just as well documented. When couples share the financial decisions rather than dividing them, ninety four percent of women report more confidence in their financial future, ninety three percent report fewer financial mistakes, and ninety one percent report less stress about money. So sit down with your spouse, more than once, and walk through all of it: where the money is, who to call, what the income will look like, what to do first. Have that conversation now, while you are both here to have it, because the version that happens after a funeral is so much harder, and so much lonelier.

Second, he could have planned for the second death, not just the first. Early in this book I asked you to build your plan around the longer of two lives. This is where that matters most. Run the numbers for the survivor alone. Make sure the plan still works, still funds a genuinely good life, when it is one person in the single brackets for fifteen years. If it only works while you are both alive, then it does not actually work.

Third, he could have defused the bomb early. Remember the last chapter. A tax-friendly plan, built with unhurried Roth conversions during the good years, is one of the kindest things you can possibly leave a survivor, precisely because the cramped single brackets hurt so much less when much of the income has already been made tax-advantaged. Sue would have felt that difference every April for the rest of her life.

Fourth, and this is the one that quietly cost Sue the most, he could have thought far harder about that pension. This one deserves its own moment, because it is where a single signature, made decades early and barely understood, echoes across twenty years of a widow's life.

When Les retired, his pension gave him a choice, the same choice most pensions offer. He could take the single-life option, which paid the largest possible monthly check but stopped entirely the day he died. Or he could take a joint-and-survivor option, which paid a noticeably smaller check every month but continued paying his widow after he was gone. Les, looking at the two numbers on the page and naturally drawn to the bigger one, chose the single-life payout. It felt like the smart move. It gave them more money every month while he was alive. What that choice actually did was trade Sue's entire future pension income for a larger check today. When Les died, the pension died right along with him, and one of the two pillars holding up Sue's income simply vanished.

Here is what almost no one standing at that retirement desk ever explains. There is a third path, and for many couples it is the best of all. It is a strategy called ***The Pension Shield Option***™, and the idea behind it is elegant. You take the larger single-life pension, the bigger check, and you use part of that extra monthly income to buy a life insurance policy on the pensioner. Now you own the best of both worlds.

While both spouses are alive, you enjoy the higher single-life payout. And if the pensioner dies first, the life insurance death benefit steps in to replace the lost pension income for the survivor, income-tax-free under current law, often more flexibly and more generously than the pension's own survivor option would ever have been. If instead the non-pensioner happens to die first, you are not locked into a permanently reduced check for a survivor who is no longer there. You simply keep your full pension and can redirect the insurance toward your children. Structured properly, ***The Pension Shield Option***™ can hand a couple more income during their joint lives and better protection for the survivor at the very same time. Les could have kept his bigger check and still left Sue completely whole. He simply never knew the option existed.

I want to be candid that ***The Pension Shield Option***™ is not automatic and it is not for everyone. It only works if the pensioner is insurable, if the insurance is adequate and permanent rather than a cheap temporary policy that expires too soon, and if the numbers genuinely favor it, which requires real analysis rather than a rule of thumb. Done carelessly, it can leave a survivor worse off than the plain survivor option would have. Done well, it is one of the most powerful moves available to anyone retiring with a traditional pension. Because this single decision is so consequential, so widely mishandled, and so specific to your own pension and your own health, I devoted an entire separate book to getting it right. If you or your spouse is retiring with a pension, please read ***The Pension Shield Option***™ before you sign a single election form. That book walks through the whole framework, wire by wire, so that the choice Les made blindly is one you get to make with your eyes wide open.

A pension election is one of the very few retirement decisions that is genuinely irreversible. There is no amendment, no do-over, no conversion later. You choose once, and your spouse lives with that choice for the rest of their life. It is worth every hour it takes to get right the first time, and it is exactly the sort of decision ***The Pension Shield Option***™ was written to keep you from getting wrong.

And fifth, *he could have made it simple.* One file. Where the accounts are, who to call, the passwords, a short letter, a clear first ninety days. Not buried in a drawer, but known. So that the person you love is never, on the worst day of her life, also completely lost.

Les Prepared loved his wife. That was never once in question. He simply did not understand that loving her meant preparing her, that the truest form of providing was not only building the wealth but building her ability to stand in it without him. *He confused taking care of everything with taking care of her.* They are not the same thing, and the difference only ever shows up on the one day he is no longer there to fix it.

You have the chance that Les did not take. Every item on that list is a way of reaching forward, past the very end of your own life, to steady the person you love most, on the day she needs it and you cannot be there. That is not estate planning. That is the last, and perhaps the finest, thing you will ever do for her.

And with that, we have named all five. The silent thief, the ambush, the long storm, the long fuse, and the one who is left. Five forces that turn a long life into a hard problem. But I want to be careful here, because a book that only names dangers is just a book that frightens people, and that has never once been my purpose. We spent all this time learning to beat these things for a reason, and the reason was never the beating. It was the life waiting on the other side of it. So let us leave the dangers behind now, all five of them handled, and spend the rest of our time together on the only question that ever truly mattered. Not how to keep the money from running out. What a long, well-funded life is actually for.

A Note on the Numbers

The financial data in this chapter is drawn from primary research rather than industry lore, because a claim this important deserves a real citation. The figures on how couples divide financial decisions, and on what widows discover only afterward, come from the UBS Own Your Worth studies. The one-third drop in Social Security set against the roughly twenty percent drop in household needs, and the jump in poverty from about four percent to about twelve percent at widowhood, come from research published by the Social Security Administration drawing on the Health and Retirement Study. The finding that widows end up with about twenty-two percent less income than widowers is from a Stanford analysis of that same study. The median age of widowhood, the fifteen-year survival figure, and the share of older women who are widowed all come from the U.S. Census Bureau. The ranking of a spouse's death as the single most stressful life event comes from the Holmes and Rahe Stress Scale.

This chapter is for general education only and is not tax, legal, or investment advice. Tax rules, Social Security provisions, and pension and insurance options are complex and apply differently to every household. Pension maximization strategies involve life insurance and depend heavily on insurability, cost, and individual circumstances; they are not suitable for everyone and can leave a survivor worse off if not properly structured. Please consult qualified tax, legal, and financial professionals regarding your own situation before making decisions about pension elections, insurance, or conversions.

CHAPTER NINE

The Smartest Person in the Room

You have just spent five chapters watching a long life turn into a minefield. Inflation that never retires. A market that ambushes you at the worst possible moment. A care event that can take the house. A tax bomb with a fuse measured in decades. And a survivor left to face all of it alone. If those chapters did their job, you are feeling two things at once. The first is a sharper sense of the stakes. The second, if you are honest, is a small, quiet question you may not much want to say out loud.

Can I really handle all of this myself?

It is one of the most important questions in this book, and how you answer it will matter more than almost any single investment you ever make. So let me tell you about the one thing that stands between most successful people and a good answer. It is not a lack of intelligence. Quite the opposite. It is a specific, well-documented trick that your own competence plays on you.

Mount Stupid

In 1999, two psychologists at Cornell, David Dunning and Justin Kruger, published a study with one of the great titles in all of social science: Unskilled and Unaware of It. They gave people tests of logic, grammar, and humor, then asked them to rate how well they thought they had done. The result was so consistent that it now carries their names: *The Dunning-Kruger Effect*. The people who scored the worst were the most confident. Not a little more confident. Dramatically so.

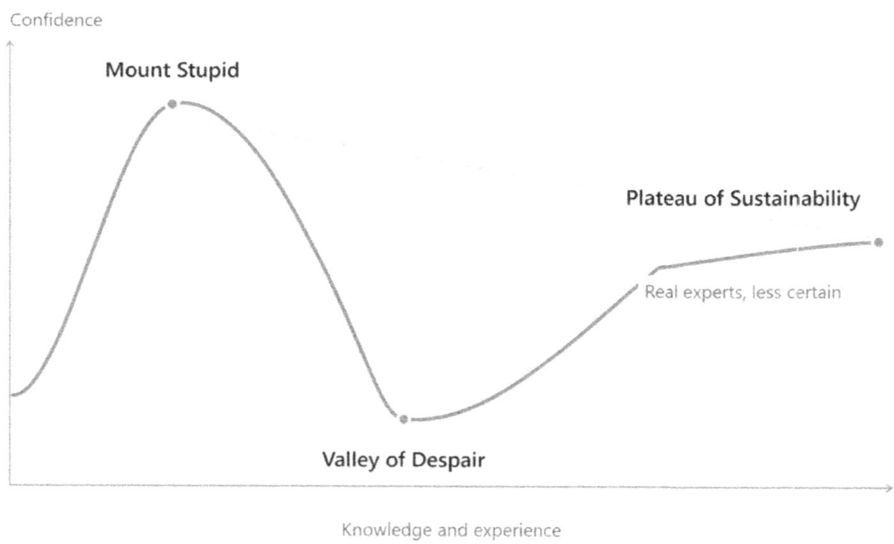

The less someone actually knew,
the more certain they were that they knew plenty.

The reason is almost poetic. The very knowledge you would need to do a task well is the same knowledge you would need to recognize that you are doing it badly. If you do not know the rules of grammar, you cannot see your own grammatical mistakes, so you sail happily along convinced you are doing fine.

Incompetence, it turns out, comes bundled with the inability to detect it.

In the years since, people have drawn the whole arc of confidence as knowledge grows, and it looks like a little mountain range. At the very beginning, knowing almost nothing, your confidence rockets to a peak that has been affectionately nicknamed Mount Stupid. Then, as you actually start to learn the subject, something humbling happens. Your confidence falls, because you finally know enough to see how much you do not know. Only much later, after genuine expertise, does confidence climb back, and even then it never quite returns to that first reckless summit. The real experts, the people who truly know, are almost always less certain than the beginners who do not. Keep that picture in your mind, because you are about to stand at the base of that mountain, whether you realize it or not.

Two Different Games

Here is why all of this matters enormously for you, specifically, at this exact moment in your life.

For thirty or forty years, you played a game called accumulation, and you may well have played it beautifully. The rules of accumulation are wonderfully simple. Earn. Save as much as you can. Buy diversified investments. Hold them. When the market falls, do nothing, or buy more. Ignore the noise. Repeat for decades. Those few plain virtues, practiced with discipline, are most of what it takes to build real wealth, and you have every right to be proud of having practiced them.

But the day you retire, the game changes, and it does not merely change a little. It becomes a different game entirely, with different rules, played on a different board. It is called decumulation, and here is the thing almost no one says out loud: you have never played it before. Not once. You have spent your whole financial life putting money in. Now, for thirty-five years, you have to take it back out, in the right order, from the right accounts, at the right time, without ever running dry. That is the game this entire book has been about. Sequence risk. Tax timing. Roth conversions and the gap years. Medicare surcharges and Social Security taxation. Funding care. Protecting the survivor. Which dollar to spend first and which to spend last. Those are the rules of the new game, and almost none of them were part of the old one.

And here is the cruelest part of all. Some of the very instincts that made you a champion at accumulation will actively hurt you at decumulation. Remember Buck and Penny, who fled to cash because holding steady had always felt so safe? That instinct built their nest egg, and then quietly began shrinking it. Remember Betty, whose buy-and-hold discipline was a genuine superpower right up until the day she had to sell into a falling market simply to eat? The reflexes that won the first game can lose the second. Being an expert at accumulation does not make you a novice at decumulation. It makes you something more dangerous than a novice: it makes you a confident one.

Why the Smartest People Are the Most at Risk

Now put those two ideas together, Dunning and Kruger's mountain and the two different games, and you can watch the trap close on precisely the kind of person reading this book.

You are, in all likelihood, genuinely excellent at something. You built a company, or ran a division, or mastered medicine, or law, or engineering. You spent a career being the competent one, quite often the most competent one, the person everyone else turned to for the answer. That is real, and it is earned. But it creates a very specific vulnerability, because deep competence in one field feels, from the inside, exactly like general competence. The brilliant surgeon, the sharp litigator, the engineer who can model anything, all carry the same quiet and entirely understandable assumption: I am smart. I figure hard things out for a living. I will figure this out too.

Let me introduce you to Dr. Noah Little. Noah was, for thirty years, one of the finest cardiac surgeons in his city. Steady hands, brilliant mind, and a confidence his patients found deeply reassuring, because you very much want a confident surgeon. When Noah retired, he approached his own financial plan exactly the way he approached the operating table: I am highly intelligent, this is important, and I will handle it myself. And he did handle it, in the sense that he personally made every decision. He also left his largest accounts untouched and untaxed well into his seventies, missed the entire Roth conversion window, sold investments in a panic during one ugly year, and chose the pension option that maximized his own monthly check. Noah knew a very great deal about the human heart and, as it turned out, very little about decumulation, though you could not possibly have convinced him of the second part. He was not a fool. He was an expert, in the wrong field, and far too accomplished to notice the difference.

Now contrast him with Willy B. Rich, every bit as intelligent as Noah, who did the one thing Noah could never quite bring himself to do. Willy assumed, going in, that a thirty-five year decumulation was a real specialty he happened to have never studied, and he treated it accordingly. That single assumption, that he might not be the expert in this one particular room, is the whole difference between the two men. It is also, and this is no coincidence, the unmistakable mark of someone standing well past Mount Stupid.

What a Guide Is Actually For

Let me be very clear about what I am and am not saying here, because the case for getting help is badly misunderstood, usually because it is so often sold badly.

I am not saying you need someone to pick better stocks. We spent two whole chapters establishing that essentially no one, not the smartest fund managers alive, reliably beats the market over time, so paying anyone to try is a loser's bargain. If that is what an advisor is selling you, keep your money and walk away.

The value of a real guide in retirement has almost nothing to do with picking investments and almost everything to do with playing the decumulation game well. It is the tax coordination, sequencing your withdrawals across accounts so that the IRS takes the smallest possible bite over the span of decades. It is the conversions, done in the right years, in the right amounts. It is managing the reserve so that a bad market never forces your hand. It is threading Medicare and Social Security so that one stray dollar does not tip you over a cliff. It is protecting the survivor. It is taking all five of the dangers in this book and weaving them into a single, coordinated plan instead of five separate worries that keep you up at night. No single page of that is beyond a smart person's understanding. But all of it, coordinated correctly, year after year, adjusting as laws and markets and your own life keep changing, is a genuine profession, not a weekend project.

And then there is the part that even the most brilliant do-it-yourselfer simply cannot do for himself, which is to be his own steady hand.

What an Advisor Is Actually Worth

Vanguard puts the value of good advice at roughly THREE PERCENT in net returns, every year.

And the single largest piece of that value is not tax strategy or investment selection. It is BEHAVIORAL COACHING.

Not a clever trade. Not a hidden loophole. Just the plain, unglamorous act of stopping a good person from doing something rash at the worst possible moment.

Morningstar's research on retirement income lands in a similar place, finding that a well-structured, tax-smart withdrawal strategy can wring meaningfully more usable income out of the very same pile of savings. The numbers matter, but the reason behind them matters more. Even geniuses panic. Even the disciplined get scared. A surgeon does not operate on his own child, and a lawyer who represents himself, as the old line goes, has a fool for a client, not because either one lacks the skill, but because each one lacks the distance. Emotion and high stakes are the exact conditions under which a second set of trained, unpanicked eyes is worth the most.

The Wisest Thing a Smart Person Can Say

So here is the reframe this entire chapter has been building toward, and it is the very opposite of an insult to your intelligence. It is a compliment to it.

The single wisest thing an intelligent person can say, standing at the start of a thirty-five-year game they have never once played, is this: I am smart enough to know that I am not the expert in this particular room. That sentence is not weakness. It is the precise sound a person makes when they have finally climbed down off Mount Stupid and can see the whole mountain at last. The most dangerous retiree I ever meet is not the one who knows nothing. It is the one who did brilliantly for thirty years and is therefore utterly certain the next thirty work the same way. The safest is the one accomplished enough to be humble about a game they have not yet played.

So here is what to do with all of this.

First, notice your own confidence, and be honestly suspicious of it in exactly those areas where you have never actually been tested. Competence in your career is not competence in decumulation, no matter how powerfully it feels as though it should be.

Second, separate the two very different jobs an advisor might do for you. If someone is selling you the ability to beat the market, that is your cue to leave. If someone is offering to coordinate the tax, income, risk, care, and survivor pieces into one coherent plan, and to be your steady hand on the day your own nerve fails, that is the job that is genuinely worth paying for.

Third, if you do decide to go it alone, at the very least go in knowing which game you are *actually* playing, and study the new rules as seriously as you once studied your own career. This book is a start. It is not a substitute for a plan built around your real numbers.

And fourth, whatever you decide, decide it on purpose, with your eyes wide open, and not out of a quiet, unexamined assumption that being brilliant in one arena makes you brilliant in all of them. Because it does not. And the people who most need to hear that sentence are precisely the ones most certain it could not possibly apply to them.

You now know the five dangers, and you know the one quiet trick your own mind plays that keeps smart people from taking them seriously. What you do not yet have is the thing that answers all five at once. A structure. A machine, built for exactly this purpose, that turns a lifetime's pile of savings into a paycheck that lasts as long as you do. That is what we build next.

This chapter is for general education only and is not investment, tax, or legal advice. Estimates of the value added by financial advice, including figures published by Vanguard and Morningstar, are research approximations based on particular assumptions and do not represent a guarantee of any specific result; individual outcomes vary. Choosing whether and how to work with a financial professional is a personal decision that should be based on your own circumstances.

CHAPTER TEN

The Income Machine

For your entire working life, retirement was a number. A single, growing figure at the bottom of a statement, the thing you were building toward. And for all those years, bigger was simply better. A larger number meant a safer future, and the whole game was to make it grow.

Then you retire, and something strange happens to that number. It stops being a source of comfort and quietly becomes a source of dread. Because now you have to live off it, and a pile of money you have to live off for thirty-five years is a genuinely frightening thing to own. Every dollar you spend is a dollar gone. Every market dip feels like the floor giving way. The very size that reassured you for forty years now only raises the stakes of every decision. How much can I safely take? What if I take too much? What if I live longer than I planned, or the market falls, or both?

This chapter is about the machine that makes that fear go away. Not by making the number bigger, but by turning it into something else entirely. A paycheck.

A Pile Is Not a Plan

Here is the core problem, stated plainly. A pile of money and a paycheck are two very different things, even when they hold the exact same dollars.

A pile is undifferentiated. It is one big number, and every part of it feels equally exposed to every risk at once. When the market drops, the whole pile seems to drop with it. When you need to spend, you are reaching into the very same pile you are terrified of depleting. There is no logic to which dollar does what, so every single dollar carries all of the anxiety. This is how you get Buck and Penny Pincher, who have more than enough and still cannot bring themselves to spend it, splitting the early bird special while sitting on a small fortune. They do not have a spending problem. They have a pile problem. Nobody ever turned their pile into a paycheck, so the whole thing just sits there radiating risk, and they ration against it out of a fear they could never quite name.

A paycheck is the opposite. A paycheck is calm. You lived on one your whole working life, and you never once lay awake wondering whether it would show up. It arrived on a schedule, in a known amount, and you spent it without guilt because you knew another one was coming right behind it. The single greatest thing you can do for your retirement, and for your own confidence, is to stop owning a pile and start owning a paycheck. The machine that performs that conversion is the beating heart of a real retirement plan, and it is simpler than you might think.

Three Buckets, Three Jobs

The machine I build, and the one at the center of the Wealthcare approach, works by flatly refusing to treat your money as one pile. Instead, it sorts every dollar into one of three buckets, each with a different job and, most importantly, a different time horizon. We call them Safety, Income, and Growth.

The first bucket is Safety, and it holds the near future. This is roughly the next two to four years of your spending, held in cash and other stable, boring instruments that do not lurch when the stock market does. This is the money you actually live on. It is deliberately dull, and its dullness is the whole point. You may recognize it, because you have met it already. It is the same reserve, the same seawall, that we built back in the chapter on the ambush, the thing that means a bad market never forces you to sell at the bottom. Here, in the machine, that seawall finally has a name and a permanent job.

The second bucket is Income, and it holds the middle distance, call it years three through ten. This is money invested more conservatively than the stock market but more productively than plain cash, in things that tend to hold steadier and produce income along the way. Its job is not to be spent directly. Its job is to refill the Safety bucket as you draw it down, so that the paycheck never stops. This is also the natural home for a tool like the buffered growth we discussed earlier, which aims to capture part of the market's gain while cushioning its drops, which is exactly the temperament you want in the middle layer.

The third bucket is Growth, and it holds the long future, the money you will not touch for ten, twenty, or even thirty years. This bucket is invested for genuine growth, which means primarily in equities, because we settled long ago that over a long horizon, stocks are the only long-run answer to the silent thief of inflation that history supports. And here is precisely why this bucket can afford to be bold: it has time. It does not care about this year's headlines or next year's crash, because it will not be called upon for decades, and decades are exactly the timeframe over which the market has historically rewarded the patient. Its job is to grow, and eventually to refill the Income bucket, keeping the whole machine running for as long as you live.

How the Paycheck Machine Runs

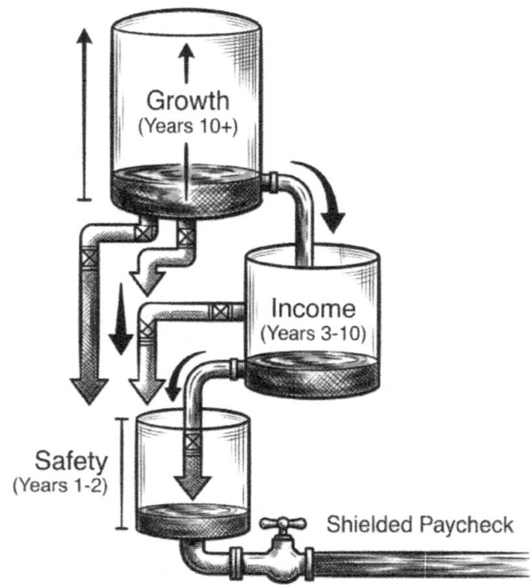

Now watch the machine actually work, because the beauty of it is in the motion.

In an ordinary year, you *spend* from the ***Safety bucket***. That is your paycheck. As it draws down, you refill it from the ***Income bucket***, and you top up the Income bucket from the gains in the ***Growth bucket***. Money flows quietly from the long buckets toward the near one, *from Growth to Income to Safety to your checking account*, and you get to live your life without ever once staring at the whole pile at the same time.

Then comes a bad year, and this is where the machine earns its keep. The market falls, sometimes hard. In a pile, that is a crisis, because you are still pulling your living expenses out of investments that are dropping by the day. In the machine, it is a shrug. You simply keep spending from the Safety bucket, which did not fall because it was never in the market to begin with, and you leave the Growth bucket completely alone to do what growth investments do after a fall, which is to recover on their own schedule. You do not sell a single share at the bottom. You do not have to. That is the seawall from the ambush chapter, now doing its permanent work inside the machine, and it is the single most important reason the whole structure holds. It converts a bad market from an emergency into a non-event.

When good times return, as historically they have, you refill the buckets from the top down and carry on. The machine breathes in and out with the market, while you, standing at the near end of it collecting your steady paycheck, barely feel the weather at all.

One Machine, Every Danger

Step back now and notice what this single structure has quietly pulled off, because it is a good deal more than it first appears.

It has answered the silent thief, because the Growth bucket is built to outrun inflation across the decades. It has answered the ambush, because the Safety bucket means a bad market never forces your hand. Those were the two dangers that pulled against each other for the entire first half of this book, the need to grow set squarely against the need not to sell at the wrong moment, and the machine dissolves that tension by simply handing each need its own bucket. Near-term money stays stable. Long-term money grows. You are no longer forced to choose between them, because you are no longer treating a thirty-five-year problem as though every dollar in it had the very same job.

And the machine is far more than a defense against two dangers. It is the chassis that holds the entire rest of the plan together. The tax strategy from the defuse chapter decides which accounts feed which buckets, so that your dollars arrive in the most tax-efficient order. The care strategy from the storm chapter sits alongside it as its own lightening rod, so that a long illness never has to drain the buckets you built for a long life. And the whole coordinated structure is exactly the sort of thing a survivor can actually be handed and keep running, rather than a mystery she is left to decode alone in the worst week of her life. This is what a real plan looks like. Not a pile, and not a pile with a few good ideas bolted onto the side, but a single machine in which every part has a job and the parts all work together.

This, by the way, is the coordination we talked about in the last chapter, the actual work that a good guide does. Anyone can grasp the idea of three buckets in a single afternoon. Building yours around your real numbers, choosing exactly what belongs in each, deciding which accounts to draw from in which order for the smallest possible tax bill, and then calmly refilling the whole thing year after year as markets and laws and your own life keep shifting underfoot, is the profession. The buckets are simple. Running the machine well, for thirty-five years, is anything but.

What the Machine Really Gives You

Let me close on the one thing the machine gives you that has nothing at all to do with money, because it is the thing that matters most.

It gives you permission.

When your income arrives as a paycheck instead of a pile, you can finally spend it. Not recklessly, but freely, and without that low background hum of dread that follows everyone who is quietly rationing against a single undifferentiated number they do not fully understand. You can take the trip. You can pick up the check. You can be generous with the people you love while you are still here to see their faces, rather than leaving it all behind out of a fear that your own plan never actually justified. Buck and Penny never got that permission, and so their fortune bought them a lifetime of splitting entrees. The machine is the very thing that would have set them free.

So here is what to do.

First, stop looking at your savings as one big number. It is not one number. It is three buckets, with three jobs and three different time horizons, and the moment you begin to see it that way, half the fear quietly drains out of it.

Second, fill the Safety bucket first, two to four years of your spending, in stable assets, before anything else gets decided. That is your paycheck and your seawall, and it is the thing that lets everything else in the machine take the long view.

Third, let the Growth bucket actually be growth. It has decades ahead of it. Do not shortchange your future self by parking your long money where your short money belongs, which is the precise mistake that lets the silent thief win in the end.

Fourth, refill from the top down in the good years, and in the bad years, spend from Safety and leave Growth entirely alone. Never be a forced seller. The whole machine exists so that you never have to be one.

And fifth, get real help building it and running it, because this is exactly the coordinated, decades-long work that is worth a professional's steady hand, and getting the order of operations wrong is an expensive way to learn.

You came into this book with a pile and a quiet fear that it might not last. You now hold the blueprint for a machine that turns that pile into a paycheck built to outlive you. Which means the question that has haunted every page so far, the one that asks whether the money will last, finally has an answer. And once that question is truly settled, a far better one is waiting behind it, the question this entire book has been driving toward since its very first page. Not whether your long life is funded. What on earth it is for.

This chapter is for general education only and is not investment, tax, or legal advice. A bucket, or time-segmented, income approach is one strategy among several. It involves investment risk, including possible loss of principal, and it does not guarantee income, ensure a profit, or ensure that your assets will last for any particular length of time. The right structure depends entirely on your individual circumstances. Please consult a qualified financial professional before implementing any strategy.

CHAPTER ELEVEN

What the Years Are For

Years ago, my longtime mentor Nick Murray said something to me that I have never once forgotten, and that I have come to believe may be the single most important sentence in all of retirement planning. We were talking about clients, and about what actually makes a retirement good, and Nick said this:

> ***"George, all of the great goals of life arise after you answer one question:"***
>
> ***"Am I going to live longer than my money, or is my money going to live longer than me?"***

Read that again, slowly, because it quietly reorganizes everything.

For ten chapters, this book has been answering Nick's question. The silent thief, the ambush, the storm, the fuse, the survivor, and the machine that turns your pile into a paycheck, all of it, every single page, has had one job: to make certain that your money outlives you, rather than the other way around. And if you have done that work, or even firmly resolved to do it, then something remarkable has just happened. You have cleared the prerequisite. You have answered the one question that stands in front of every other question. Which means that, for perhaps the first time in your life, you are free to ask the ones that *actually* matter.

Because here is the quiet truth that Nick understood. Nobody has ever lain on their deathbed wishing they had spent more time optimizing their withdrawal sequence. The money was never the point. The money was only ever the ticket of admission. And this book would be a failure, and I would have genuinely wasted your time, if all it did was make sure your long life was funded without ever once asking what that long, funded life is actually for.

The Man Who Retired the Title

Let me tell you about a danger this book has not yet named, and it is one that money cannot touch, because it strikes hardest at the people who have plenty of it.

You have spent thirty or forty years being someone. The surgeon. The founder. The captain. The partner. The person whose opinion mattered, whose calendar was always full, whose title told the world, and told you, exactly who you were. For most successful people, the work and the self grew up together over the decades until it became genuinely hard to say where one ended and the other began. Your identity and your occupation quietly fused into a single thing.

And then you retire, the title comes off, and a great many accomplished people discover, to their private horror, that they no longer know who they are without it. The phone stops ringing. The problems that used to require you now get solved just fine by someone else. The competence that defined you suddenly has nowhere to go. This is not a small thing, and it is not rare. Researchers who study retirement find that for people whose entire identity was bound up in their work, retirement can bring a real and measurable slide into depression and aimlessness, and in the hardest cases an actual decline in health, not because they ran out of money, but because they ran out of reasons to get out of bed in the morning.

The cruelty of it is exquisite, and it is the exact shape of this entire book. The extra decade you fought so hard to fund, the reward waiting at the end of a long and successful life, can curdle into the emptiest stretch of that life, if you arrive at it having carefully planned every dollar and not a single day. You cannot retire from your career and retire from your purpose in the very same week and expect to be happy. One of those two things has to be replaced.

Two Ways to Waste a Fortune

You have already met two people who show you precisely how this goes wrong, and it is worth seeing them clearly one last time, because only now can we name what actually ails them.

Buck and Penny Pincher have the money. By now they have even built the machine, so the paycheck arrives on schedule and the old fear should be long gone. And still they cannot bring themselves to live. They drive the extra fifteen minutes for cheaper gas, split the entree, and let the trips they always talked about slip past one more year, and then one more year after that. We used to say that Buck and Penny had a pile problem. But underneath the pile problem was always something deeper. Buck and Penny never decided what the money was for. So even with permission finally granted, they have nowhere to spend it, because spending requires a vision of the life you are spending toward, and they never once built one. Their tragedy is not that they will run out of money. It is that they will run out of time with a fortune still sitting untouched in the bank, having purchased almost nothing that ever mattered to them.

And then there is Al Nighter, who fails in the opposite direction entirely. Al retired, but Al never actually stopped. He is still awake at three in the morning watching the foreign markets, still managing, still optimizing, still treating his portfolio as the main event of his life. Al did not carry his career into retirement because he loved the work. He carried it in because it was the only thing he knew how to do with himself, and an empty calendar frightened him far more than a falling market ever had. So he filled the extra decade with the one activity that still felt like purpose, which was tending money he did not need, and he called it retirement. Al is not enjoying his freedom. He is hiding from it.

Buck and Penny cannot spend the money. Al cannot stop minding it. They look like opposite problems, and they are in fact the very same problem. Not one of the three of them ever answered the question this chapter is about. Not one of them knows what the years are for.

Purpose Is Not a Luxury

Here is the part that should change how seriously you take all of this, because it turns out that purpose is not a soft, optional, greeting-card sort of thing. It is closer to medicine.

Some of the longest-lived people on earth live on the island of Okinawa, and they have a word, ikigai, that roughly translates as the reason you get out of bed in the morning. It is not a hobby, and it is not a bucket list. It is a felt sense that your days are for something. And when researchers went looking, they discovered that this was no coincidence. Across large and careful studies, a strong sense of purpose in life turns out to be associated with living longer, staying mentally sharper, and holding off disability and decline. In one major study of older Americans, those with the weakest sense of purpose were found to be markedly more likely to die over the years that followed than those with the strongest, even after accounting for wealth, health, and nearly everything else.

Now sit with what that means alongside everything this book has already told you. The extra decade is real. You are genuinely likely to get it. And the single best thing you can possibly put inside it, the thing that will make those years both richer and, quite possibly, longer, is a real reason to be alive in them. Purpose does not merely fill the extra years. It may help you earn more of them. Which means the work of figuring out what your long life is for is not something to get around to eventually, once the financial planning is finished. It is the financial planning, finally paying off.

So let us do that work now, on the page, with an exercise I give the people I care most about helping. It takes half an hour and a quiet room, and it may be the most valuable half hour in this entire book.

"A definite purpose, backed by a burning desire,

is the starting point of all achievement."

NAPOLEON HILL

An Exercise: The Extra Decade Daydream

Before you begin, sit for a moment with a single question. What would your life look like if every part of it were working at once? Picture great energy and vibrant health, the kind that lets you say yes without first asking whether your body can keep up. Picture rich, connected relationships, the people who matter close and present. Picture peace and order in your days, with nothing nagging at you and nothing chasing you. And picture an abundance of wealth, enough that money has become a quiet servant rather than a loud master. Hold that whole picture for a moment. That is the life the extra years are for. Now let us go and find them.

1. The invisible finish line. Without overthinking it, write down the age you quietly assume you will reach. Name it, because a number you have never actually examined has been steering your decisions all along.

2. Move the line. Set that number against the evidence from Chapter 1. The very traits that made you successful have almost certainly drawn your finish line ten to fourteen years too early. The gauge was simply wrong.

3. Live one ordinary day inside the extra years. Relax, close your eyes, and walk slowly through one vivid, unremarkable, perfect day deep in that added decade. See it. Hear it. Feel it as though it has already happened to you.

4. Feel the gratitude. The emotional charge is the engine of the whole thing. Feel grateful for those years as if you have already lived them. Gratitude is what fuels the progress toward the dream, and the deeper the gratitude, the faster it seems to come.

5. Write it down. This is the magic key. Capture what you saw, and heard, and felt, and you move the dream out of the part of the brain that merely imagines it and into the part of the brain that actually gets things done.

6. Claim one now. Name a single thing from that daydream that you will begin this month, not someday. The extra years are not a distant reward to be collected later. They become yours the moment you decide to start living them.

7. Fund the drive. A daydream is only a wish until something pays for it. Take one thing you saw in that perfect day and hand it to the machine we built in the last chapter. Put it on the calendar, and put it in the budget. That is the exact moment your plan stops being about not running out of money and starts being about the life the money was always for.

Do not rush this, and do not do it once and file it away. The people who get the most out of a long life are the ones who revisit that daydream, refine it, and keep pulling pieces of it forward into the present, one claimed thing at a time.

Let me tell you why this exercise means so much to me, because it is more personal than any technique. That picture you just built, a compelling vision of the years ahead, is the very first thing my firm exists to help people create. When someone asks what we actually do, I answer with a single sentence, and it is the truest one I know how to say about my work:

Our mission is to help successful people create compelling visions of their futures; the plans to attain them and the time and enduring wealth to enjoy them.

Read it slowly, because it is also, from its first word to its last, the shape of this entire book. The vision is the daydream you just wrote. The plans are everything in the chapters that came before it. And the time and enduring wealth to enjoy it all is the long, well-funded life you now know how to build. This book, in the end, is simply that mission, written down.

I will confess one small vanity here, and then set it back down. That mission statement, and the years of thinking that went into arriving at it, was compelling enough that the *Financial Times* chose to feature it. For someone who started out with very little, that is a strange and humbling thing to be able to say. But the recognition was never the point, and it never is. The point is the work, and the lives it exists to serve. Yours among them.

Back to Nick's Question

Come back now to Nick Murray's sentence, because you are finally standing on the far side of it. Am I going to live longer than my money, or is my money going to live longer than me? You have answered it. The machine answers it. And Nick's promise was that once you do, all of the great goals of life arise. Not some of them. All of them. The travel and the grandchildren and the causes and the second acts and the quiet, ordinary Tuesdays worth getting out of bed for, every one of them was patiently waiting on the far side of that single question, and you have just walked through the door.

So do not waste the room you are now standing in. You did the hard, unglamorous work of making sure the money would last. Now do the harder, and far more important, work of making sure the life is actually worth it.

There is one movement of this symphony left to play, and it is the most beautiful one. Because a life with its money solved and its purpose found is still missing one last thing, a way of holding it all together into something whole, and a way of letting it spill over, while you are still here, onto the people who come after you. That is where we end.

CHAPTER TWELVE

The Symphonic Life

For most of my life, I chased a balanced life. You have probably chased it too. It is the great modern promise, the one on every magazine cover and in every wellness seminar: get all the pieces of your life level, the work and the family and the health and the money and the rest, hold them all in perfect equilibrium, and you will finally be at peace.

I no longer believe in the balanced life. I have come to think it is a quiet lie, and that chasing it makes people miserable, because life simply does not work that way. A perfectly balanced life is a life in which everything is always the same, and nothing is ever fully alive. Watch anyone who has actually done something beautiful, raised a child, built a company, come back from a devastating loss, and you will not find balance. You will find seasons. Times when one thing rightly consumed nearly everything, and other times when it receded to let something else take the stage.

What I believe in now is a symphonic life. In a symphony, the instruments do not all play at the same volume all the time. That would not be music. It would be noise. The strings swell and then fall quiet so the horns can rise. A single flute carries an entire passage alone. The whole orchestra goes silent for one held breath, and then everything comes crashing back together for the finish. It is not balanced. It is composed. The genius of it is in which elements play, at what intensity, at which exact moment, so that across the full length of the piece, something magnificent gets built.

> *"To everything there is a season, and a time to every purpose under the heaven."*
>
> ECCLESIASTES 3:1

That is what a long, well-planned life can be. Not a flat, balanced ledger of evenly divided days, but a symphony, with room and time and money enough to let each movement have its turn. The extra decade you have spent this whole book learning to fund is not a quiet coda tacked onto the end. It is whole movements you did not know you would get to play. And I want to spend these last pages on how to make them beautiful. To do that, I have to tell you where the music in my own life came from.

A Boy in the Projects

I began life in the public housing projects of South Philadelphia, in a place called Wilson Park. We were poor in the plain, unglamorous way that poor actually is. I remember the end of the month, when the money ran thin, and dinner was a mustard sandwich, two pieces of bread and a smear of yellow mustard, because that was simply what there was. I was bullied as a kid, small and scared, and I did not look, to anyone including myself, like a boy who was going anywhere in particular.

But I had a daydream. In that daydream I was strong, and I was capable, and I was, someday, going to have enough. Enough money, enough safety, enough strength and skill, enough courage to protect the weak and the innocent, enough of a life that a mustard sandwich at the end of the month would be a story I told and not a thing I feared. I did not have a plan. I was a kid in the projects. But I had the picture, and I held onto it.

Now here is the part I need you to sit with, because it is the whole reason I am qualified to write this chapter, and maybe this entire book. That daydream came true. All of it. The boy eating mustard sandwiches went on to graduate first in his class from the state police academy, to serve his country, to save more than a dozen lives with his own two hands, a police self-defense instructor, to stand at podiums in places like Oxford and Cambridge and the London Stock Exchange, and to build a life of real and lasting abundance. I am not telling you that to impress you. I am telling you because I am living, breathing proof of the single most important thing I know: dreams really do come true. Not by magic. But they come true far more often for the people who dare to hold the picture than for the people who never once let themselves draw one.

The Fall, and the Look Up

But I would be lying to you, and this book has never lied to you, if I let you believe the road ran straight.

There came a point, after the years in public safety, after everything I had seen and carried, and after building a high level of success after I transitioned to banking, when my life came apart. The details are mine to keep, but the shape of it will be painfully familiar to anyone who has ever been knocked flat: a collapse, a loss, a stretch of time where I was, by any honest measure, wiped out, genuinely unsure I would get back up.

In that stretch, I remembered what the great speaker Les Brown had told me when we met at a conference, something I have carried with me and frequently shared ever since:

> ***"If you are going to fall, fall on your back — because if you can look up, you can get up."***

I was on my back. And so, with very little else left to me, I did the only thing I had ever known to do when I had nothing. I closed my eyes, and I daydreamed. I built the picture of the life I wanted, in vivid detail, as if it had already happened. I let myself feel exactly what it would feel like. My body and my mind overflowed with gratitude. And then I wrote it down.

That half hour, and the many like it that followed, turned my life around one hundred and eighty degrees. Not overnight, and not without an enormous amount of work. But in retrospect, it happened quickly enough that there could be no other logical explanation. Within two years I was living that life. After ten years, my life had expanded so far it was unrecognizable.

But the turn began in that daydream, in the deliberate act of building a picture of a better life and feeling grateful for it before it had arrived. The exercise I gave you in the last chapter is not some technique I read in a book. It is the thing that saved my life, handed to you.

So when I tell you that the extra decade can be the best part of your life, understand that I am not offering you a pleasant theory. I am telling you what I have personally lived, too many times to count. Once as a bullied boy with a mustard sandwich, and more than once as a grown man on his back, looking up. The picture, the gratitude, the writing it down. It works. I am the evidence.

Let me make that one word, evidence, as concrete as I possibly can. Back in the early nineteen nineties, when I was struggling to raise a family and financially and emotionally support my parents and siblings, I kept what I called an aspirations file, a folder of pictures of the life I intended to build. One of those pictures was a house. Not a home I owned, or could remotely afford, or had any earthly reason to believe I ever would. Just a photograph of a place that looked the way I wanted my whole life to feel, clipped and saved and looked at from time to time. In the year 2020, nearly twenty-five years later, I moved into that house. My dream home, the very one from the folder. I am writing these words inside it.

The boy from Wilson Park who ate mustard sandwiches at the end of the month now enjoys a seven-figure income and lives in the million-dollar dream home he first met as a photograph two and a half decades before he ever held its keys. I do not tell you that to impress you, and I would ask you not to read it that way. I tell you because it is the most *literal proof* I know how to offer that the exercise in the last chapter is no party trick. I pictured it. I wrote it down. I let myself feel exactly what it would be like to live there. And then, slowly, and through an enormous amount of work, it came true, right down to the house. And if I had understood sooner that it is the power of gratitude, not the power of desire, that gets you there fastest, I am certain it would not have taken twenty years.

You Only *Die* Once

Now let me hand you the reframe that changes what you actually do with all of this, because there is a slogan loose in the world that I think has it exactly backwards.

You have heard it. YOLO. You Only Live Once. It is usually shouted as an excuse to be reckless, to blow the money, to do the foolish thing, on the cheerful theory that life is short so you may as well.

But it is wrong, and not in the way people think. *You do **not** only live once.* You live every single day. You only ***die*** once. That is the thing that happens a single time, right at the very end. Life is not the one rare event. Life is the ten thousand ordinary days in between, and you get to live every one of them. That single reframe changes everything, because if life is the daily thing and not the final thing, then the question is no longer how to survive until the end. It is how to actually live, on purpose, all the way through.

And it changes what legacy means, which is the last big idea I want to leave you with. Most people think of legacy as something that happens after they die. It is the will, the inheritance, the question of who gets your leftover stuff once you are finished using it. I want to offer you a better definition, one that fits a life you live every day rather than die once at the end of. Your legacy is not the stuff you leave behind. ***Your legacy is the experiences and the feelings you create along the way, in the people whose lives touch yours.*** It is how your grandchildren felt at your table. It is the trip your family will still be telling stories about in thirty years. It is what the world got to become because you were in it. That legacy is not written in a will. It is written every single day, in real time, by how you actually choose to spend the life you are living right now.

Giving with Warm Hands or Cold Hands?

This leads to the most practical, and perhaps the most beautiful, piece of advice in the whole book, and it came to me not from a textbook or investment conference but from a client. Her name is Eileen, one of the very first financial planning clients I ever had, back in 1996. During a recent end of year estate planning review, she said something to me that I have often repeated and will never forget.

George, she told me, "I want to give with warm hands, not cold hands."

Sit with that for a moment. Cold hands are the hands of the departed. Giving with cold hands is the traditional way, the inheritance that arrives only after you are gone, the check your children open when your hands can no longer hold anything at all. It is not wrong, and there is real love in it. But Eileen had seen something deeper. She understood that if she waited to give until her hands were cold, she would never get to see any of it. She would never watch her beneficiaries open the thing, never see her gift change the course of a life or the missions she endowed, never feel the warmth of the very moments she had made possible.

Warm hands are the hands of the living. Giving with warm hands means giving now, while you are here, while you can still see the faces and feel the joy and be part of the story. It means helping your children with the house while you can watch them raise their own family inside it, funding the education while you can sit at the graduation, taking the whole family on the trip while everyone is still young enough to remember it forever. This is why we did all the hard, unglamorous work of the earlier chapters. We did not build a plan to last your whole long life so that you could die with the largest possible pile.

We built it so that you could give, and spend, both money and time, and love with warm hands, generously and confidently, for decades, and still have plenty left over.

A well-funded long life is not a fortune to be guarded. It is an overflowing cup, and the entire point of an overflowing cup is that it spills onto the people standing around it.

The Horizon You Finally Stand On

Which brings me, at the very end, back to gratitude, because it is where the music started and it is where it has to finish.

For your whole life, the good life was somewhere out ahead of you, on the horizon, that place off in the distance where the earth and sky meet. When I make partner. When the kids are grown. When the mortgage is finally paid. When I have enough. You spent decades walking toward that horizon, and the strange, cruel trick of any horizon is that it always recedes, staying forever just ahead of you, no matter how far or how fast you walk.

Here is what this book has really been about, underneath all the strategy. You are now standing on that horizon. The place where the earth and sky meet is just beneath your feet. The place you spent your entire life walking toward, you have arrived at. The *enough* you always chased, you now have. The long life you feared you could never afford, you *can*. The question is no longer how to get to the good life. You are already in it. The only question left is whether you will let yourself notice.

Gratitude is how you notice. It is the simple, almost radical act of looking around at the life you spent forty years building and letting yourself feel that it is good, that it is enough, that you actually made it. Not someday. Now. The people who suffer most in retirement are almost never the ones with the least money. They are the ones who arrive at the horizon they chased their whole lives and cannot stop scanning the distance for the next one. Do not be that person. You have run the race. Let yourself, at long last, enjoy the view.

And from that place, *standing on the horizon,* grateful and secure, ask yourself the one question that a life this fortunate is really for. Not how much more can I possibly get. But how will the world be a little better because I was here. Answer that question with your warm hands, across all the years you now finally know how to fund, and you will not have merely avoided the longevity trap. You will have composed something. A symphony. A life that used every instrument, at the right moment and the right intensity, and built, across its whole long and astonishing length, something magnificent.

That is the extra decade you did not know was coming. Not a liability to be funded. A gift to be played.

Go and make it beautiful.

CONCLUSION

The Scenic Route

When we started, I told you about a retirement book gathering dust on a shelf in your house, quietly propping up the short leg of a workbench, and I promised you that this one would be different. I hope, all these pages later, that it was.

We have traveled a long way together. We began with a single, unsettling fact, that you are very likely to live far longer than you ever planned for, and we followed that one fact everywhere it led. Into the five dangers that a long life quietly amplifies. Through the tools and the structure that beat every one of them. And out the far side, into the only questions that ever truly mattered, the ones about purpose, and gratitude, and what a long life is actually for.

I want to leave you with the image I have carried the entire time, the one sitting underneath every chapter. Your retirement is a drive. And for most of your life, someone sold you the wrong version of that drive, the one where the only goal is to arrive, where you keep your eyes locked on the destination and your knuckles white on the wheel and you try to get there with just enough left in the tank.

*That is **not** a life. That is a **commute**.*

The road turned out to be far longer than you were told. And a long road with your eyes fixed only on the horizon is its own kind of misery. But a long road, on which you have finally understood that the drive itself was always the point, is very nearly the greatest gift a person can be handed. That is the scenic route. Not the fastest way to the end, but the fullest way through the middle, with time to pull over, and the windows down, and the people you love in the car, and the whole astonishing view rolling past.

You now know how to fund that drive for every last one of its extra miles. You know how to keep the silent thief out of your wallet and the ambush out of your plan. You know how to build a paycheck that lasts as long as you do, and how to protect the one who is left behind. And you know, I hope, the thing that matters more than all of it combined: that the money was never the point, that the years are for living and not merely surviving, and that the good life you spent so very long chasing is the one you are standing squarely inside of right now.

So here is my last word to you, and it is the same one I would give a dear friend heading out on the trip of a lifetime.

The road is longer than you were told. You have made sure you can afford every mile of it.

Now roll the windows down. And enjoy every single one.

ACKNOWLEDGMENTS

No book is the work of one person, and this one least of all. It exists because of the people who taught me, freed me, sharpened me, and believed in me, often before I fully believed in myself.

Over the past decade I have had the great fortune to learn from an extraordinary group of business coaches and mentors: Nick Murray, Dan Sullivan, Bill Good, Dan Cuprill, Scott Keffer, Clint Arthur, Deidre Van Nest, Becky Ruby Swansburg and Erin Botsford. Each of them, in their own way, pushed me to reach further than I thought I could and handed me strategies I still use every day. And I owe a special and lasting debt to my longtime mentor, E.R. Haas, whose influence runs quietly through everything I do. If these pages carry any wisdom at all, much of the credit belongs to them. My own shortcoming was never a lack of ideas or ambition. It was execution.

Which is why I owe so much to the remarkable team I have built over the last two years, the group I affectionately call George's Angels: Renee Adkins, Rosemarie Toole, and Eva Cincuite. By lifting the weight of clerical and operational work off my shoulders, they gave me something priceless, the freedom to spend my hours where they mattered most, on research and writing. And in that same vein my handyman-helper, Anthony LaVerghetta, kept my house and grounds from falling down around me while I read and typed. The proof of what they made possible now sits on a shelf: three books that reached number one bestseller status across ten categories in 2026. That was their achievement as much as mine.

I am deeply grateful to Mark Cacciatore, my friend and chief manuscript reviewer and proofreader, whose careful eye made this book and several others better on every page. And I want to thank Glenn Trotter, the finest compliance reviewer I have ever worked with, a man who genuinely knows his craft and who, rather than simply shutting a project down, always took the time to show me how to do it correctly instead. Every author in this industry should be so fortunate.

I also want to acknowledge my high school English teacher, Joanne Clothier. I had several wonderful English teachers in high school and in college, and every one of them told me I had a talent worth developing. But Joanne was something more. She was an extraordinary teacher, genuinely kind, and deeply encouraging, and at a moment in my life when I really needed someone to give me a break, she did. Writers remember those people. I have never forgotten her.

And to my old friend Dave Bontempo, whom I have known since first grade and who has walked beside me through twelve years of school, the friendship of a lifetime that does not require constant contact to remain real. Dave and Mary Fran are among the most respectful, loyal, and quietly admirable people I know. They are leaders not just by title but by example, and they have faced some of life's most difficult chapters with a grace and a courage that has inspired everyone around them. Mary Fran is a gifted writer and an inspiring public speaker. I am proud to know them both.

Last, and most certainly not least, I thank Michelle Mullin, my CEO, my Chief Encouragement Officer. She gave me steady encouragement when I needed it, space when I needed that instead, and with her incredible financial acumen, gave the honest challenge I needed most of all. Every writer should have a Michelle in their corner.

To all of you, my deepest thanks. This book is yours as much as it is mine.

George McReynolds

ABOUT THE AUTHOR

George McReynolds, CFP®, has spent his entire life defending people. He only changed *how* he was defending them.

He began in the Wilson Park public housing projects of South Philadelphia, the first-born son of seven children, poor in the plain way that poverty actually is, and bullied often enough that he resolved early to become someone who protects and defends the weak and innocent and *also* masters money. He did both. For a decade he served as a decorated Army MP, a paramedic, self-defense trainer and a SWAT officer, saving more than a dozen lives with his own hands, assigned to the security detail of the Supreme Allied Commander at NATO, working in the emergency room at Landstuhl Army Medical Center, and graduating first in his class from the Pennsylvania State Police Academy while completing paramedic certification at night.

Then he turned from defending lives to defending wealth. After leaving public safety in 1985, George entered banking, where a rare ringside seat from private banking referrals taught him how affluent families actually manage, and mismanage, their money. He earned his CFP® designation, opened a tax practice, and worked every corner of the tax system, from blue-collar returns prepared in half-hour blocks to complex planning for business owners and high-net-worth families with a CPA firm. Recruited to a prestigious Main Line investment firm, he went on to guide more than a thousand pharmaceutical employees and retirees through the tangle of retirement, taxes, employee benefits and stock compensation, the work that became his life's specialty.

Today George is the Founder and CEO of McReynolds & Company, LLC, and a best-selling author whose books include *Defuse the Bomb*, *The Pension Shield Option™*, *Stop, DROP and Roll*, *Prosperity by Design*, and *Uncle Joe's Gems*. He has spoken at Oxford University, the Royal Society of Medicine, the London Stock Exchange, the Harvard Club of Boston, and the FBI Academy National Association, and has been featured on CNN, in the *Financial Times*, *Business Insider*, *Yahoo! Finance*, and on the cover of *Philadelphia Life Magazine*.

But George has never believed money is the point. A certified life coach, clinical hypnotherapist, NLP Practitioner and Master Trainer in time management, the originator of the Life-Chain Theory and a five-time firewalker with Tony Robbins, he has spent as many years studying how people flourish as how they fund it. That rare pairing is the whole reason for this book. He wrote *The Longevity Trap* because too many accomplished, disciplined people plan carefully for a twenty-year retirement and then live thirty-five, funding the arithmetic of a long life while forgetting to compose the life itself. His work, in the end, is what it has always been. He is still defending people. Only now it is their whole long lives he is looking after.

Appendices

Appendix A: The Math Behind the Magic Trick

Appendix B: Constance Gaines and Upson Downs: Why the Smoother Ride Wins

Appendix C: The Flashlight and the Crystal Ball: A Plain-English Guide to Monte Carlo Analysis

Appendix D: A Short History of the Shrinking Dollar

Appendix E: The Odds Behind the Trap

Appendix F: The Cast of Characters: One Last Roll Call

Appendix A

The Math Behind the Magic Trick

In the chapter on sequence of returns risk, you met Willy B. Rich and Betty Wont, and I asked you to believe something that sounds impossible: two retirees with the same million dollars, the same withdrawals, and the exact same list of annual returns can end up living opposite lives, decided entirely by the *order* in which those returns arrive. Almost nobody believes it the first time. This appendix exists so you do not have to believe it. You can check it.

Here are the ground rules of the illustration. Each retiree starts with $1,000,000 at age 65. Each withdraws $50,000 at the beginning of every year to live on. Whatever remains is then invested for the year and earns that year's return. The twenty-five annual returns are identical for both retirees, the very same list of good years and bad years. Willy receives them in one order. Betty receives the same list in exactly the reverse order. That is the only difference between them.

Average the twenty-five returns in either column and you get the same number twice: 7.0 percent. Even the compound growth rate of the two return lists is identical, because reversing the order of multiplication never changes the product. By every summary statistic an accountant would compute on the returns themselves, these two retirements are the same retirement.

Now watch what happens.

Willy B. Rich: The Good Years Come First

Year	Age	Withdrawal	Return	Year-End Balance
1	65	$50,000	24%	$1,178,000
2	66	$50,000	17%	$1,319,760
3	67	$50,000	14%	$1,447,526
4	68	$50,000	21%	$1,691,007
5	69	$50,000	10%	$1,805,108
6	70	$50,000	28%	$2,246,538
7	71	$50,000	13%	$2,482,088
8	72	$50,000	15%	$2,796,901
9	73	$50,000	-6%	$2,582,087
10	74	$50,000	18%	$2,987,862
11	75	$50,000	9%	$3,202,270
12	76	$50,000	16%	$3,656,633
13	77	$50,000	4%	$3,750,899
14	78	$50,000	13%	$4,182,015
15	79	$50,000	-8%	$3,801,454

Year	Age	Withdrawal	Return	Year-End Balance
16	80	$50,000	10%	$4,126,600
17	81	$50,000	7%	$4,361,962
18	82	$50,000	12%	$4,829,397
19	83	$50,000	3%	$4,922,779
20	84	$50,000	-12%	$4,288,045
21	85	$50,000	6%	$4,492,328
22	86	$50,000	-20%	$3,553,862
23	87	$50,000	5%	$3,679,056
24	88	$50,000	-15%	$3,084,697
25	89	$50,000	-9%	$2,761,575

Willy finishes the year he turns 89 with $2,761,575, nearly triple the million he started with, and sails into his nineties still withdrawing $50,000 a year. His rough stretch arrived, and it was every bit as ugly as Betty's: look at the last six years of his table. But by then the storm was beating against a portfolio of several million dollars with most of his retirement already behind him.

Betty Wont: The Same Years in Reverse

Year	Age	Withdrawal	Return	Year-End Balance
1	65	$50,000	-9%	$864,500
2	66	$50,000	-15%	$692,325
3	67	$50,000	5%	$674,441
4	68	$50,000	-20%	$499,553
5	69	$50,000	6%	$476,526
6	70	$50,000	-12%	$375,343
7	71	$50,000	3%	$335,103
8	72	$50,000	12%	$319,316
9	73	$50,000	7%	$288,168
10	74	$50,000	10%	$261,985
11	75	$50,000	-8%	$195,026
12	76	$50,000	13%	$163,879
13	77	$50,000	4%	$118,434
14	78	$50,000	16%	$79,384
15	79	$50,000	9%	$32,028

Year	Age	Withdrawal	Return	Year-End Balance
16	80	*$50,000 needed*	18%	**Only $32,028 remains**

Betty withdraws the identical $50,000 every year and earns the identical returns, just in reverse order. Her retirement opens with the bear market Willy did not meet until his eighties. She spends her first six years selling shares at depressed prices to raise grocery money, and by age 70 the portfolio has already lost the engine it needed. When she reaches for her withdrawal at 80, only $32,028 remains against a $50,000 need. She spends her early eighties rationing what is left.

And here is the cruelest line in the entire table. The return posted for Betty's final year is +18 percent. The recovery showed up right on schedule. She simply had almost nothing left for it to recover. Every strong year that follows in her list, and there are many, belongs to the part of the sequence she never lived to invest in. That is sequence of returns risk in a single column of numbers: the market gave Betty everything it gave Willy, and the order took it away.

What This Table Is Telling You

The average return of a portfolio tells you how the investments performed. It does not tell you how the retiree performed, because a retiree who is withdrawing income does not experience the average. She experiences the order. This is why the years immediately before and after your retirement date, called *the red zone*, carry more weight than any other years of your investing life, and why the planning for that window deserves more care than any other planning you will ever do.

Important disclosure: This is a hypothetical illustration and is not representative of any specific investment or strategy. The returns shown are hypothetical, do not reflect the performance of any actual investment, and do not include fees, expenses, or taxes, which would reduce results. This illustration assumes fixed annual withdrawals of $50,000 taken at the start of each year with no adjustments for inflation or changing circumstances. It is intended solely to demonstrate the concept of sequence of returns risk. Past performance is no guarantee of future results. Investing involves risk, including the possible loss of principal.

Appendix B

Constance Gaines and Upson Downs: Why the Smoother Ride Wins

Willy and Betty taught you that the order of returns can defeat the average. This illustration teaches the companion lesson: the size of the swings can defeat the average too. Meet Constance Gaines and Upson Downs, two more retirees with the same million dollars and the same $50,000 annual withdrawal, taken at the start of each year with the remainder invested for the year.

This time the returns are not identical. Upson earns the higher average, 8 percent a year across the decade. Constance averages only 6 percent. If retirement were decided by the average, this would not be a contest. Ask yourself, honestly, which retiree you would rather be, then look at the tables.

Upson Downs: The Higher Average

Year	Age	Withdrawal	Return	Year-End Balance
1	65	$50,000	-13%	$826,500
2	66	$50,000	-20%	$621,200
3	67	$50,000	5%	$599,760
4	68	$50,000	-7%	$511,277
5	69	$50,000	20%	$553,532
6	70	$50,000	25%	$629,415

Year	Age	Withdrawal	Return	Year-End Balance
7	71	$50,000	-25%	$434,561
8	72	$50,000	45%	$557,614
9	73	$50,000	30%	$659,898
10	74	$50,000	20%	$731,878

Upson's decade averages a genuine 8 percent, and it includes some spectacular years, up 45, up 30, up 25. It also includes the other kind, down 25, down 20, down 13, and every one of those bad years forced him to sell shares at depressed prices to raise his $50,000. Ten years in, the man with the winning average is down to $731,878. His portfolio never got to compound in peace.

Constance Gaines: The Smoother Ride

Year	Age	Withdrawal	Return	Year-End Balance
1	65	$50,000	6%	$1,007,000
2	66	$50,000	8%	$1,033,560
3	67	$50,000	7%	$1,052,409
4	68	$50,000	11%	$1,112,674
5	69	$50,000	-4%	$1,020,167
6	70	$50,000	6%	$1,028,377

Year	Age	Withdrawal	Return	Year-End Balance
7	71	$50,000	12%	$1,095,783
8	72	$50,000	-2%	$1,024,867
9	73	$50,000	10%	$1,072,354
10	74	$50,000	6%	$1,083,695

Constance never has a year within shouting distance of Upson's best. Her single finest year, up 12 percent, would rank fifth on his list. What she has instead is an absence of disasters: her worst year is a modest 4 percent dip. Averaging two points less per year, she finishes the decade at $1,083,695, ahead of where she started and $351,817 ahead of Upson.

Why the Average Lies

Two forces are working against Upson, and both hide inside that flattering 8 percent.

The first is pure arithmetic, and it would hurt him even without withdrawals. A portfolio that drops 25 percent needs a 33 percent gain just to break even, so big swings quietly compound to less than their average suggests. Run the two return lists with no withdrawals at all and Upson's 8 percent average compounds at only about 5.6 percent a year, while Constance's 6 percent average compounds at about 5.9. Her boring returns outgrow his exciting ones before a single dollar is withdrawn. Statisticians call the gap volatility drag. Retirees call it the years they cannot get back.

The second force you already know from Willy and Betty: withdrawals turn temporary declines into permanent ones. Every

$50,000 Upson pulled during a down year was raised by selling shares at fire-sale prices, shares that were never there for the 45 percent year that followed. Volatility digs the hole, and withdrawals throw the shovel in after it.

A useful way to picture the difference in the two rides: statistically, roughly two years out of three, Upson's annual return landed somewhere between 14 percent down and 30 percent up, a 44-point corridor of possibility. Constance's typical year landed between 1 percent up and 11 percent up. One of these retirees checked her balance with her morning coffee. The other checked his with his cardiologist.

What This Table Is Telling You

In the accumulation years, when you are adding money and spending nothing, volatility is survivable and sometimes even your friend, because your contributions buy shares cheap in the bad years. In the distribution years, the arithmetic reverses and volatility becomes a direct tax on your lifestyle. This is why a retirement portfolio is not simply an investment portfolio with grayer hair. It is a different machine, built for a different job: converting savings into a paycheck that survives both the order of returns and the size of the swings. Upson Downs beat Constance Gaines on average. Constance beat Upson in every year that mattered.

Important disclosure: This is a hypothetical illustration and is not representative of any specific investment or strategy. The returns shown are hypothetical, do not reflect the performance of any actual investment, and do not include fees, expenses, or taxes, which would reduce results. This illustration assumes fixed annual withdrawals of $50,000 taken at the start of each year with no adjustments for inflation or changing circumstances. It is intended solely to demonstrate the effect of return volatility on a portfolio in distribution. Past performance is no guarantee of future results. Investing involves risk, including the possible loss of principal.

Appendix C

The Flashlight and the Crystal Ball

A Plain-English Guide to Monte Carlo Analysis

in Retirement Distribution Planning

Why This Appendix Exists

Earlier in this book you met Willy B. Rich and Betty Wont, two retirees with the same million dollars, the same withdrawals, and the same returns, separated only by the order in which those returns arrived. One sailed into his nineties. The other ran dry in her early eighties. If that story taught you anything, it taught you this: the average return tells you almost nothing about whether your money will last. The order is everything.

That creates a problem for planning. If the order of returns matters this much, and nobody on earth can predict the order, how do you plan at all?

The financial planning profession's best answer to that question is a technique called Monte Carlo analysis. You will almost certainly encounter it if you work with any competent advisor, and you deserve to understand what it is, what it does well, and where it quietly falls short. That is what this appendix is for.

What Monte Carlo Analysis Actually Is

The name comes from the famous casino district in Monaco, and the name is honest: the method is built on randomness.

A traditional retirement projection works like a ruler. It assumes your portfolio earns the same return every single year, say seven percent, marching in a perfectly straight line from your retirement date to your final birthday. Draw the line, check whether the money lasts, done.

You already know why that ruler lies. A straight-line projection does not just simplify the order of returns. It erases the order entirely. Betty Wont's straight-line projection looked identical to Willy's. It told her she was fine. She was not fine.

Monte Carlo analysis throws away the ruler. Instead of running your retirement once with an average return, the software runs your retirement hundreds or thousands of times. Each run is a different simulated lifetime. In one, the market crashes the year you retire. In another, you get a roaring bull market for a decade and then a slump. In another, returns zigzag with no pattern at all. Each simulated lifetime draws its yearly returns at random, based on assumptions about how markets tend to behave, and each one plays your plan forward: your withdrawals, your timeline, your portfolio, tested against a different possible ordering of good and bad years.

Then the software counts. If your money lasted in 870 of 1,000 simulated lifetimes, your plan is said to have an 87 percent probability of success.

In other words, Monte Carlo analysis takes the magic trick from this book seriously. It does not ask, "What happens if you earn the average?" It asks, "What happens across a thousand different orderings, including the ones where you get Betty's luck?"

What Monte Carlo Does Well

Used properly, Monte Carlo analysis makes three genuine contributions to your retirement.

First, it respects sequence of returns risk. This is its whole reason for existing. A straight-line projection cannot see Betty coming. A Monte Carlo simulation contains hundreds of Bettys, because hundreds of the simulated lifetimes begin with a bear market. If your plan survives most of them, that tells you something a ruler never could.

Second, it replaces false certainty with honest probability. A straight-line plan gives you a yes or a no, and both answers are overconfident. Monte Carlo gives you a range. It teaches you to think the way the future actually works: not "I will be fine" or "I am doomed," but "under most reasonable futures, this plan holds."

Third, and most valuably, it shows you your levers. The real power of the tool is not the number it produces. It is what happens when you change the inputs. Retire one year later and watch the success rate move. Trim spending by five percent and watch it move again. Add a guaranteed income floor and watch what happens to the worst outcomes. Monte Carlo turns retirement planning from a verdict into a conversation about tradeoffs you actually control. That conversation is where good plans come from.

Where Monte Carlo Falls Short

Now the other side of the ledger, because this tool has real limitations, and an informed retiree should know every one of them.

The assumptions drive everything. A Monte Carlo simulation is only as good as the estimates fed into it: expected returns, volatility, inflation, correlations between asset classes. Nudge the assumed stock return down by one percentage point and a plan can drop from a 90 percent success rate to somewhere in the 70s. Two advisors running the same client through different software, with different assumptions, can hand back meaningfully different probabilities. The lesson is not that the tool is useless. The lesson is that the number is an output of the assumptions, not a measurement of your future.

The precision is partly an illusion. "An 87 percent probability of success" sounds scientific down to the last digit. It is not a probability about the actual future. It is a probability inside a model of the future. The difference matters. Treat the number as a rough compass heading, not a GPS coordinate.

Markets are messier than the model. Most simulations assume yearly returns follow a tidy bell curve and that each year is independent of the last. Real markets do neither. Crashes arrive more often than a bell curve predicts, a property statisticians call fat tails. And markets show memory: bad stretches cluster, and deep declines have historically been followed by strong recoveries. A simulator drawing independent random years can understate how ugly the bad stretches get, and it can also understate the market's historical tendency to heal afterward. Reasonable experts argue about which error is bigger. Either way, the randomness in the machine is not quite the randomness in the world.

It assumes you are a robot. This may be the most important limitation in the entire list. The classic simulation assumes you withdraw the same inflation-adjusted amount every year for thirty years no matter what is happening around you. Markets down 40 percent? The robot keeps spending. But you are not a robot. Real retirees adjust.

In the good years, you take the cruise. In the bad years, you stay home and watch The Love Boat.

Many of the "failed" lifetimes in a simulation only fail because the imaginary retiree never once changed course. This is why a plan with an 80 percent success rate is often far safer in real life than it looks on paper, provided the retiree is willing and able to adapt.

The willingness to adjust is the single most powerful risk-management tool you own, and it is the one variable most simulations leave out.

All failures are not equal, but the tool counts them that way. A simulated lifetime that runs out of money at age 72 and one that runs a small shortfall at 94 both land in the failure column with equal weight. Probability of success tells you how often the plan falls short, but nothing about how badly or how soon. A more useful question is often not "what are my odds of failure?" but "if things go badly, how large an adjustment would I need to make, and when?" Some planners now frame results exactly that way, as a probability of adjustment rather than a probability of ruin, and it is a healthier way to read the output.

Real life has line items the model skips. Taxes and the order in which you tap different account types. The new roof. The long-term care event. Inflation that spikes and settles rather than marching at a constant rate. Some software handles some of these; much of it handles them crudely or not at all. The simulation tests your portfolio against market randomness, but retirement is exposed to more kinds of randomness than markets alone.

How to Read a Monte Carlo Result Like a Professional

Put the strengths and weaknesses together and a sensible way to use this tool emerges.

Start by accepting that nobody gets 100 percent. Nobody. If the richest man in the world walked into my office with a trillion dollars and told me he planned to spend one thousand dollars a year, his plan would not score 100. The future does not hand out guarantees, and an honest simulation will not pretend otherwise. Once you make peace with that, the number becomes useful, because now you can read it in zones.

Below 70 percent, you should not have confidence in your plan. The simulated futures are telling you that too many orderings of returns break it, and hoping for Willy's luck is not a strategy. Something needs to change: the spending, the timeline, the savings, or the structure of the plan itself.

Between 70 and 90 percent, you are in the comfort zone. The plan survives the large majority of futures, and the ones it does not survive are exactly the futures where a flexible retiree would adjust anyway. This is where a well-built plan should live.

And here is the part almost nobody tells you: over 90 percent at retirement, or over 95 percent in your eighties, is not a triumph. It is a warning sign pointing the other direction. It means you are living in sacrifice. You have too much money stacked at the wrong end of the plan, and the price is being paid right now, in trips not taken, experiences postponed, and generosity deferred. Remember the lesson of warm hands. A success rate that high is not telling you that you are safe. It is telling you that you are underliving your one retirement.

Ask what moves the number. The single number is the least interesting thing on the page. The interesting part is the sensitivity: what happens at one percent lower returns, at higher inflation, at a longer life, at a two-year delay, at a modest spending cut. A plan that survives the stress tests is worth more than a plan with a prettier headline number.

Rerun it regularly. A Monte Carlo result is a snapshot, not a contract. Markets move, spending changes, life happens. The projection you ran at 62 says little about your situation at 70. The tool earns its keep through repetition, as an ongoing checkup rather than a one-time verdict.

Remember what it cannot see. It cannot see your health, your family, your flexibility, or your character. It cannot see that you would rather cut a vacation than lie awake at night. Those things belong in a plan. They will never be in a simulation.

The Bottom Line

Monte Carlo analysis is a flashlight, not a crystal ball. It cannot tell you which future you will get, and anyone who says otherwise is selling certainty that does not exist. What it can do is sweep the beam across a thousand possible futures, including the dark ones, so that you and your advisor can see whether your plan survives Betty's luck and not just Willy's.

That is a genuine advance over the ruler. Just remember that the plan is not the printout. The plan is the ongoing discipline of measuring, adjusting, and course-correcting as the real future reveals itself one year at a time. The simulation assumes you will never adjust. Your greatest advantage is that you will.

Important disclosure: Monte Carlo simulations are hypothetical illustrations based on assumptions about future market behavior. They are not predictions or guarantees of future results, do not reflect actual investment performance, and actual results will vary. Probabilities of success are model outputs and should not be interpreted as the actual likelihood of any outcome. This material is for educational purposes only and is not intended as specific investment, tax, or legal advice. Investing involves risk, including the possible loss of principal. No strategy assures success or defends against loss in a declining market.

Appendix D

A Short History of the Shrinking Dollar

Sequence of returns risk can wreck a retirement in a decade. Inflation works differently. It has never wrecked anyone's retirement in a decade. It prefers thirty years, moving so slowly you rarely feel it, until one day the paycheck that once felt generous will not cover the life you built it for. Betty Wont went broke because of the order of her returns. But even a retiree who dodges Betty's luck faces this second adversary, the patient one, and it has a perfect record: it has shown up in some strength in every long retirement in American history.

Everything in this appendix comes from one public source: the U.S. Consumer Price Index, the government's official measure of prices, as maintained by the Federal Reserve Bank of Minneapolis in a table running from 1913 through the present. Since that record began, the overall price level in America has multiplied roughly 32 times over. A dollar from 1913 does the work of about three cents today. That is an average of about 3.2 percent per year, compounded across more than a century. Keep that number in mind. It is the quiet drumbeat under everything that follows.

The Dollar You Were Born With

The most personal way to see inflation is to ask what has happened to the dollar over your own lifetime. The table below shows, for each birth year, what it takes today to buy what $1,000 bought the year you arrived, along with the average annual inflation rate across your lifetime.

Born in	What $1,000 then requires today	Your lifetime average inflation
1940	$22,993	3.8% per year
1945	$17,883	3.7% per year
1950	$13,357	3.5% per year
1955	$12,011	3.6% per year
1960	$10,875	3.7% per year
1965	$10,219	3.9% per year
1970	$8,296	3.9% per year

Read your row twice. If you were born in 1955, prices have multiplied twelvefold in your lifetime, and nobody sent you a bill. The increase arrived a few percent at a time, in years that mostly felt normal. That is the signature move: inflation does its damage in years when nothing seems to be happening.

A Century in One Table

Averages hide the plot, so here is the story decade by decade, each figure the compound annual inflation rate for that stretch.

Decade	Average inflation	What was happening
1920s	-1.8%	Prices actually fell
1930s	-1.7%	Depression-era deflation

Decade	Average inflation	What was happening
1940s	5.6%	War and postwar surge
1950s	2.1%	The long calm begins
1960s	2.7%	The calm starts to crack
1970s	7.8%	The Great Inflation
1980s	4.7%	The fever breaks, slowly
1990s	2.8%	The quiet returns
2000s	2.4%	Quiet, with a crisis
2010s	1.7%	The quietest decade of modern times
2020s so far	4.5%	The spike nobody under 60 had ever seen

Three chapters of that table deserve a closer look, because your retirement will be shaped by which chapter you silently assume comes next.

The Great Inflation, 1973 to 1981. If you are reading this book, you probably lived through it. Inflation ran 6.2 percent in 1973, then 11.1, and by 1980 hit 13.5 percent, the worst year of the era. In the eight years from 1973 to 1981, the overall price level more than doubled. Think about what that sentence means for a retiree on a fixed income: the same pension check, the same bond interest, and everything at the store costing twice as much before a single decade had passed. An entire generation of retirees learned this lesson the hard way, and it is the reason your parents' generation talked about inflation the way coastal towns talk about hurricanes.

The long quiet, 1983 to 2020. Then came nearly four decades of calm, mostly 2 to 3 percent, bottoming out in the 2010s at under 2. This is the chapter that trained today's retirees. If you formed your money habits between 1990 and 2020, low inflation feels like the natural order of things, the way the world simply is. The table says otherwise. The quiet was one chapter, not the whole book.

The reminder, 2021 and 2022. And then, in two years, the quiet ended: 4.7 percent in 2021 and 8.0 percent in 2022, the hottest single year since 1981. Nothing about that episode was historically unusual. That is precisely the point. What was unusual was the forty-year stretch that preceded it. The 2022 spike was not the exception to the rule. It was the rule, briefly visible again.

What This Means for a 30-Year Retirement

Now put the century's average, roughly 3 percent, inside a retirement that the longevity tables say you should plan to fund for 25 to 30 years. The arithmetic is not complicated, and it is not kind.

Suppose it costs $100,000 a year to live the retirement you want. At 3 percent inflation, that same life costs about $134,000 in year ten, $181,000 in year twenty, and $243,000 in year thirty. Nothing about your lifestyle changed. Only the price tag did.

Or run it in reverse, which is how a fixed income experiences it. A pension or payout locked at $100,000 a year still buys $100,000 of living on the day you retire. By year thirty, at that same 3 percent, it buys about $41,000 worth. Not because anyone took anything from you. Because you stood still while prices walked.

This is why the word "safe" is the most dangerous word in retirement income. An income that cannot grow is not safe. It is merely certain, and certain of the wrong thing: certain to buy less every single year, through every chapter of whatever inflation history gets written next. A retirement plan does not merely need income that lasts as long as you do. It needs income that grows as long as you do. How to build that kind of income is what the rest of this book is about.

Source and disclosure: All price data are annual average Consumer Price Index figures (CPI, and CPI-U from 1978 forward) as published by the U.S. Bureau of Labor Statistics and compiled by the Federal Reserve Bank of Minneapolis, 1913 through 2025. Decade and lifetime averages are compound annual rates calculated from those annual averages. The projections at 3 percent inflation are hypothetical illustrations, not predictions; actual future inflation will differ and may be higher or lower. Past inflation is no guarantee of future price levels. This material is for educational purposes only and is not intended as specific investment, tax, or legal advice.

Appendix E
The Odds Behind the Trap

This book's title makes a claim: that living a long time, the thing every one of us hopes for, is also a trap for the unprepared. A claim like that should not rest on a feeling. It should rest on arithmetic. This appendix is the arithmetic.

The Most Misleading Number in Retirement Planning

Ask most people how long they will live and they will quote a life expectancy figure, something in the low-to-mid eighties for a 65-year-old today. Then they quietly plan as if that number were a deadline. It is not a deadline. It is a midpoint. Roughly half the people who reach 65 will outlive their life expectancy, some of them by a decade or two. Planning your money to last exactly to the average is not caution. It is a coin flip, and it is a coin flip you lose by living.

The actuarial profession, whose entire job is measuring how long people live, has built a free public tool to make this visible: the Actuaries Longevity Illustrator, created by the American Academy of Actuaries and the Society of Actuaries. Instead of one number, it shows the odds of reaching each age. The shape of those odds is what most retirement plans get wrong. Consider a healthy, nonsmoking 65-year-old woman. The illustrator gives her roughly a 73 percent chance of reaching 85, a 53 percent chance of reaching 90, a 29 percent chance of reaching 95, and a 10 percent chance of blowing out one hundred candles. Read that middle number again: for a healthy woman retiring today, reaching 90 is not the long shot. It is the better-than-even bet. A healthy man's odds run somewhat lower at every age, but the same shape holds.

The Couple's Coin Flip

Now the number this book is named for. Most retirements are not planned for one life. They are planned for two, and the mathematics of two lives is stranger than most people expect, because the plan does not end when the first spouse passes. It has to last as long as the second one, and nobody knows in advance which spouse that will be or how long they will go.

For a married couple, both 65, drawn from general population mortality tables used by the Social Security Administration:

For a 65-year-old couple, the chance that...	is roughly...
At least one spouse lives past 90	1 in 2
At least one spouse lives to 95	1 in 5

A coin flip that one of you sees 90. Around one chance in five that one of you sees 95. And notice the trick in the mathematics: the couple's odds are better than either spouse's individual odds, because the couple gets two chances at longevity. Two people who each have modest odds of a very long life combine into a household that probably contains one. This is the single most under-appreciated fact in retirement planning, and it is why a couple's plan built to each spouse's individual life expectancy is quietly underbuilt for the household's actual risk.

Your Odds Are Probably Better Than These

One more turn of the screw. The couple's odds above come from general population tables, which average together everyone: every health condition, every income level, every smoker. If you are the kind of person reading a retirement planning book, you are probably not average. Higher incomes, more education, better access to healthcare, and nonsmoking status are each associated with longer lives, and the actuarial tools show it: run a healthy, nonsmoking couple through the Longevity Illustrator and the odds of a 90th and 95th birthday in the household climb well above the population figures. The very traits that put this book in your hands are the traits that make its title your problem.

What the Odds Demand of a Plan

Planning researchers who have studied this question arrive at a consistent answer: for a typical 65-year-old couple, a planning horizon of roughly 30 years, to age 95, is the reasonable baseline, not the cautious extreme. Not because you are guaranteed to get there, but because the odds that the household does are far too high to ignore, and the consequence of being wrong in that direction, meaning alive and broke, is the one retirement outcome with no recovery plan.

Hold this appendix next to the others and the full shape of the trap appears. The longevity tables say the household should plan on roughly three decades. The inflation record says that over three decades, the cost of your life roughly doubles and then some. And Willy and Betty showed that across a stretch that long, the order of returns can quietly decide everything. Long life is the multiplier on every other risk in this book. It is also, let us not forget, the prize. The entire purpose of the planning in these pages is to make sure that when your 90th birthday arrives, and for one of you it probably will, it arrives as a celebration and not as a bill you cannot pay.

Source and disclosure: Individual survival probabilities are drawn from the Actuaries Longevity Illustrator (longevityillustrator.org), a free public tool developed by the American Academy of Actuaries and the Society of Actuaries, for a nonsmoking 65-year-old in good health; results vary by age, sex, health, and smoking status. Couple probabilities reflect Social Security Administration period life table data and are rounded. All figures are statistical estimates for large groups, not predictions for any individual, and mortality data are updated over time. This material is for educational purposes only and is not intended as specific investment, tax, or legal advice.

Appendix F

The Cast of Characters: One Last Roll Call

Every character in this book was invented to carry one lesson, because a lesson wearing a name and a face outlives a lesson wearing a chart. Here is the whole cast, each with the one line they would want on their business card. If you remember nothing else from these pages, remember them. They will introduce themselves again the next time you are tempted to make their mistake.

Willy B. Rich. Retired into a bull market, got the good years first, and never fully appreciated that the difference between his retirement and Betty's was luck of the calendar, not brilliance.

Betty Wont. Earned the very same returns as Willy in reverse order and ran dry in her early eighties. She is the reason this book takes the order of returns more seriously than the average of them.

Constance Gaines. Never had a spectacular year in her life and won anyway. Proof that in retirement, the smoother ride beats the higher average.

Upson Downs. Beat Constance on average and lost to her in every year that mattered. His 8 percent was more exciting than her 6, and considerably more expensive.

Norm. A man who was above average in every measurable way and planned for the middle anyway, with a spreadsheet that stopped at 80. The trap is named after people like Norm.

Buck and Penny Pincher. Saved so carefully they forgot to live, permanent residents of the sacrifice zone. Their money will outlast them by decades, which is not the compliment it sounds like.

Al Nighter. Lost a thousand nights of sleep worrying about his money instead of building a plan that would have let him rest. Worry is not a strategy, and it pays no interest.

Sue Vivor. The one the plan was really for all along, because every couple's plan is ultimately tested by whichever spouse remains to live on it.

Les Prepared. Was absolutely going to get around to it. The most expensive sentence in retirement planning is next year.

Mel Thusela. Outlived every projection anyone ever ran for him, cheerfully. The best argument in this book is that you might be him.

Dr. Noah Little. Brilliant in his own field and dangerous in his own portfolio. He knew just enough to be confident, which is the most expensive amount of knowledge there is.

And one real person.

Eileen. A client since 1996, and the source of the line this entire book is reaching for: it is better to give with warm hands than with cold ones. The fictional characters spend these pages learning what she already knew.

The characters above are illustrative; please see the Characters and Examples note in the front of this book.

Made in United States
Orlando, FL
15 September 2026

87759400R00121